THE GREAT JOURNEY

AN ALLEGORY

BY JOHN ROSS MACDUFF

EDITED BY CHRISTIAN HORSTMANN

Carmel Cove Publications
an imprint of ChristianFamilyReformation.com

ISBN: 978-0-578-84985-0

Originally published by John Ross MacDuff as
*The Great Journey: A Pilgrimage through the Valley of Tears,
to Mount Zion, the City of the living God.*

This reprint is based upon the 1854 edition, and it has been
modified and re-typeset at the sole discretion of the Editor.

Cover photo by Roberto García Ruiz
flickr.com/photos/dobetoh/44291940284

Internal layout, editing, proofreading,
and cover design by Christian Horstmann
fivestareditingservices@gmail.com

Table of Contents

*Let your intellect be exercised concerning
the Lord Jesus. Meditate upon what you read: stop
not at the surface; dive into the depths. Be not as the
swallow which toucheth the brook with her wing,
but as the fish which penetrates the lowest wave.*

~ *Charles H. Spurgeon*

Foreword
by Dennis Gundersen

It brings me much delight to learn of Christian Horstmann's putting John MacDuff's *The Great Journey* back into print. A prolific Scottish author of the 19th century, MacDuff wrote edifying Biblical studies such as *The Prophet of Fire* (about Elijah), and *Paul's Song of Songs* (a commentary on Romans chapter 8), among many others. But when he wrote *The Great Journey,* MacDuff stepped out of his usual style to compose an allegory. Many have attempted writing in that genre – no doubt prompted by the enduring popularity of Bunyan's *Pilgrim's Progress* – but very few have done it well. MacDuff is an exception, giving readers a volume of vivid pictures of the journey of the follower of Christ from the Valley of Tears to his rest at Mount Zion. I hope *The Great Journey* enjoys a wide readership in this new edition!

Dennis Gundersen
President, Grace & Truth Books
Board Member of Tlapaneco Indian Ministries

Editor's Note
by Christian Horstmann

Two years ago, when I first came across an original copy of the book that you now hold in your hands, I knew that this was something that had to be placed back on the bookshelves of the people of God. I was familiar with some other writings of Mr. MacDuff, which are excellent works indeed; but this particular work is one-of-a-kind. If you've fallen in love with John Bunyan's *Pilgrim's Progress,* you'll immediately feel like you're on familiar – although slightly different – territory. The author, I believe, has done a great job in portraying the great journey of one whom we might very properly call the brother of Bunyan's Pilgrim, Christian. After all, the spiritual progress of no two Christians is exactly identical; although there are experiences and circumstances that are very much the same from pilgrim to pilgrim, there are also encounters and incidents that are very different. That is why I emphasize that this book is *not* a replacement for Bunyan's classic – indeed, I would not even wish such a thing. Rather, I hope that it will earn the privilege of becoming a companion volume that occupies a side-by-side position with *Pilgrim's Progress* – similar to the manner in which we, as individual Christians, ought to stand shoulder-to-shoulder as a complement and encouragement to one another.

I would like to express my gratitude to my parents and sisters for their encouragement and assistance, which allowed me to carry this project to completion. Many thanks are also extended to the various persons who donated their time to read through my drafts and provide sound advice and valuable feedback and suggestions. In addition, I'm supremely grateful to those individuals who supplied me with their written thoughts, which formed the foundation for the majority of the questions for thought which have been added at the end of each chapter. Above all, thanks be to the Lord God of the Christian Pilgrim, Whose Providence first put this book in my way; and Whose strength enabled me to present my reader with this finished result of many long hours of preparation and polishing. May He be pleased to use it for the blessing and encouragement of each and all who are a Pilgrim on the path to Mount Zion.

Standing by His grace,
Christian Horstmann
December 2020
Proverbs 3:5, 6

Author's Preface
by John Ross MacDuff

The author feels that every apology is needed for venturing to commit to the press another of the many faint echoes of *The Pilgrim's Progress*. He has been induced to do so from experience of the power which allegory possesses, of interesting and instructing youth. This little volume, indeed, dates both its origin and much of its present form to preparations for an advanced Sabbath-school class, where the allegorical method had proved to be pleasing and profitable. If, through the Divine blessing, this book should be made the means of conveying some practical and scriptural truths to any young inquirer; the author will then be willing to share in the censure which (not undeservedly) has fallen upon a host of imitators, whose repeated failures have only tended to demonstrate and enhance the value of the great Original – *The Pilgrim's Progress*.

In the Broad Way | 1

As I was walking along the Highway of Time, I came to a new milestone; and being wearied with my journey, "I laid me down in that place to sleep; and as I slept, I dreamed a dream."[1]

In my dream, I saw a dwelling, which was situated by itself in one of the world's secluded valleys. In front of its simple, rustic lintels, there stood an aged man – pale and agitated. His eyes were pensively fixed upon the ground; or if they were occasionally lifted to take a hurried glance at some distant object, it seemed to be a relief when he could replace them on the green grass at his feet, and resume his deep and expressive thoughtfulness. The tear which now and then involuntarily fell from his eye, told some singular tale of sadness; while the other members of the household, who were gathered around him, manifested – by word and look – how amply they shared his embittered feelings.

The appearance of their home itself, as well as what was around it, indicated nothing except happiness and enjoyment. The sunbeams, at the moment, were dancing and sparkling upon a brooklet which murmured close by. A cluster of rugged trees behind the house were casting fantastic shadows upon the grass; while birds of various kinds were responding to one another, from bough to bough, in joyous music.

While pondering the possible cause of these strange emotions, I observed someone quickly disappearing in the distance. The group surrounding the cottage door were wistfully following his footsteps. Their sorrowful words soon revealed his history. It was a member of their family, who had just bidden farewell to the home of his

---

[1] *The Pilgrim's Progress.*

youth, and commenced – all alone – upon the world's great pilgrimage! A few minutes before, his father had followed him to his threshold, with many benedictions. Warning him to "flee from the wrath to come,"[2] he had directed his footsteps to the Celestial City, whose shining gates were at the end of the path through the Valley of Tears. "My son," were his parting words, "if sinners entice thee, consent thou not... Walk not thou in the way with them; refrain thy foot from their path."[3] Full of filial love, Pilgrim (for that was the name of the traveler) had promised a dutiful obedience; and with his staff in his hand, he had set out upon his journey.

Before proceeding far, he had arrived at the edge of the forest, through which his path had led. There he found himself in an open space, in sight of two separate roads. At the entrances to these roads, crowds of wayfarers were gathered. They varied in outward appearance, but he at once concluded them to be fellow-travelers.

The footpath which he had hitherto been following terminated here, and it was necessary to select one or the other of these two ways; so Pilgrim seated himself upon a stone, close by, hesitating between the two. There was no difficulty in discovering which was the favorite. It was a broad way, without any gate at its entrance. Also, it seemed (from its appearance) to be pleasanter than the other. Shady trees were planted on either side, and the multitudes which were crowding therein seemed light-hearted and happy – with little care upon their countenances, and little sorrow in their hearts.

The adjoining way was very narrow, and it had a narrow gate at its entrance; moreover, it was frequented only by a small number – a few straggling travelers. And many of these had tears in their eyes, and burdens upon their backs.

"I can never think of joining these unhappy wayfarers," said Pilgrim to himself, as he arose and advanced in the direction of the Broad Road. And yet, as he approached nearer, he listened to sounds

---

[2] Matthew 3:7.
[3] Proverbs 1:10, 15.

to which his ear had been hitherto unaccustomed, and which made him tremble. Travelers whose names were Drunkard, Liar, Swearer, Wasteful, Infidel, and Scoffer – he found that these were to be his companions. He called to mind some words which had been impressed upon him by his father's prayers: "There is a way which seemeth right unto a man; but the end thereof are the ways of death!"[4]

Now, as Pilgrim was preparing to retrace his steps, I saw that an individual from the crowd came up and stopped him. His name was Deceiver – a well-known character to all of the Broad-way-men, and one of the most powerful vassals of the Prince of Darkness.

"How now, good traveler!" exclaimed Deceiver, with assumed gentleness. "I see that you are faint-hearted – as many before you have been – in entering this Broad Way. Tell me the cause of your fear."

"The way of the ungodly shall perish,"[5] replied Pilgrim firmly. "I had almost resolved to select it, but I see abundant reason now for preferring the other – narrow and deserted though it be. I shall, at all events, try out that narrow entrance. If it disappoints my expectations, it will be no difficult matter to retrace my steps."

"You make a mistake, ignorant youth," replied Deceiver. "Once you enter that gate, there is no possibility of turning back. That determination, once taken, can never be recalled. If you will only be persuaded to *try out* the Broad Way, there is no necessity to pursue it farther than inclination leads you."

"But how can I possibly enter with such company?" asked Pilgrim.

"Good friend," said Deceiver (still assuming a tone of kindness), "you see the worst of the way at its commencement; your companions will improve as you advance. It is only because you are not accustomed to such company that you are opposed to it. Moreover,"

---

[4] Proverbs 14:12.

[5] Psalm 1:6.

continued he, "although there is only *one entrance* to the Broad Way, there are *many footpaths* in it. If you have a dislike to those who are openly profane and vicious, there is no necessity to walk in fellowship with them. I shall introduce you to others who are more adapted to your taste."

In an unguarded moment, Pilgrim forgot his resolutions; and, under the guidance of Deceiver, he was conducted until he found himself travelling down the Broad Road.

Pilgrim thought he could not be wrong in attempting this pathway; and yet he could not forget, among the other warnings which he had received, that "many deceivers were gone out into the world."[6] But there was no room left for hesitation. Before long, he discovered that he and his guide had been unconsciously advancing, leaving the entrance at a considerable distance behind them. Deceiver, having thus accomplished his goal, returned back to exercise the same unscrupulous trickery upon others. He felt that he could confidently leave the new traveler in the hands of those who were similarly duped as himself, and had now become experienced Broadway-men. And there *was* one regard in which Pilgrim's conductor had *not* misled him. The farther Pilgrim proceeded, the less he felt the aversion (which he had experienced so strongly at first) to mingle with his fellow-travelers. His language, his manners, and his tastes – all became every day more in accordance with theirs. He even began to wonder how he could have made the selection of this road a matter of hesitation.

There were, indeed, some moments when his father's warnings were vividly recalled – particularly when he happened to be in the company of two well-known individuals in the Broad Way, with bloated faces and haggard looks, who were called Extravagance and Overindulgence. At such times, living words – with which he had been familiar since his boyhood – would often sound in his ears: "Upon the wicked he shall rain snares, fire and brimstone, and an

---

[6] 2 John 7.

horrible tempest: this shall be the portion of their cup."[7] Or again: "Come out from among them, and be ye separate, and touch not the unclean thing."[8] At these times, he would also call to remembrance how his father used to speak of a day when the Lord Immanuel was to be seated upon a Great White Throne; when before Him would be gathered all of the wayfarers who had ever traversed the Valley of Tears; and when He would say to every worker of iniquity, "Depart from me, ye cursed, into everlasting fire."[9] Pilgrim would remember how his father used to speak of the end of those who did not obey the King of the Way – and particularly of a bottomless pit at the end of a dark and deceitful road, where thousands were continually perishing without any hope of mercy. At times, this thought would flash across his mind: could it be possible that he was treading this awful highway? Being forgetful of his parents' counsels, was he was hurrying on to such certain and irretrievable ruin? The fearful possibility occasionally seemed to utterly overwhelm him – he would pause, and tremble, and weep. Or, stealing away from the boisterous merriment of his fellows, he would watch for some favorable opportunity – unseen to them – of retracing his steps.

This, however, was not an easy matter. As I have said, he had already advanced far on the way. The road which had been so broad and spacious at first, was now narrow and confined in many places. Fresh travelers were coming in; he was unavoidably carried along with the crowd, and the attempt to return would only expose him to ridicule. His companions, moreover, found that it was no difficult matter to laugh away his "fits of moping melancholy" (as they called them). And if these fits occasionally proved to be more obstinate than at other times, they always had an easy remedy at hand, by enticing him into one of the many Arbors of Pleasure that the Prince of Darkness had erected along the road. There, amidst new fascinations and carnal delights, they succeeded in dispelling his short-lived

---

[7] Psalm 11:6.

[8] 2 Corinthians 6:17.

[9] Matthew 25:41.

convictions and fears. Thus, day by day, Pilgrim was found hurrying along with the crowd – his heart growing less susceptible of feeling, with every resisted warning. The unhappy victim of a thousand corrupt passions soon had no leisure to even inquire as to where his footsteps were hurrying him. But the Pit of Destruction was at hand (although he did not know it), and he was about to be summoned to take his stand on its edge.

I saw in my dream that the shadows of evening were gathering one night, as Pilgrim found himself – weak and exhausted – at the mouth of a valley. Dangerous rocks frowned above his head on either side, and cast an ominous gloom upon the path below; while a foaming river – dark and troubled – was hemmed in between their narrow ledges. This was the Valley of Death!

As the traveler entered the Valley, a horror of great darkness came upon him. He remembered being told of a Star – the Star of Bethlehem – which gave light and peace to those passing through. He looked for it now, but in vain; and the farther he advanced, the more intense was the gloom. The ground began to heave under his feet. Peals of thunder echoed on every side. The lightning's momentary glare only served to show him that he was on his way to Outer Darkness! Upon reaching the end of the valley, he witnessed – straight before him – columns of smoke and flame, issuing from the mouth of a bottomless pit! Groans – resembling the cries of dying men – were also carried to his ears. "Verily, there was but a step between him and death!"[10]

"What shall I do to be saved? What shall I do to be saved?" exclaimed the agonized man, making a hopeless effort to retrace his footsteps. But, from his weakness, he sunk powerless to the ground. Awful was the spectacle which then presented itself! Hundreds around him were tumbling over the precipice – uttering wild curses! Others, who were already in the pit, were sending up the vain entreaty for a single drop of water to cool their tongues. "O God! Have mercy!" they cried. "Save us from this place of torment!

---

[10] 1 Samuel 10:3.

Our punishment is greater than we can bear!" But Pilgrim had no time to gaze upon the scene. The crowds from behind were pressing him nearer to the brink every moment! And he, too, would have been thrown headlong into the flames; if there had not been a ledge of projecting rock within his reach, which he grasped in the agonies of death. As he continued to thus tremble by the side of the abyss, an individual with a dark and gloomy countenance approached him. His name was Despair, and a smile of devilish triumph was seated upon his lips.

"Well, good traveler," said he, addressing Pilgrim; "you have well-nigh reached the end of your journey. There is now but one step between you and perdition; and the quicker that step is made, the better for yourself!"

"Oh! Wretched man that I am!" exclaimed Pilgrim, uttering a shriek of agony. "Is there no one who can deliver me from this abyss of death? If you have any compassion on a miserable soul, tell me – is there no possible way of deliverance from such torments?"

"None! None!" replied Despair. "There never was a traveler before you who ventured to ask such a question. The moment you entered that Valley, your Eternity was lost!"

"Nay," said Pilgrim, who was so stupefied with terror that he was scarcely able to collect his thoughts to reply. "I think I once heard of one who was undone like myself. He was called Malefactor, and he stood where I am now – on this dreadful precipice. And just as he was about to plunge in, he cried out in imploring accents, 'Lord, remember me!' Immediately, a golden chain of grace was let down from heaven; and that same day, he was with Jesus in Paradise."

"That is only some dream of your own, unhappy traveler," said Despair. "If you had thought of returning as you journeyed through the wilderness, or before you came in sight of the Valley of Death – some hope might have remained. But now, all possibility of escape is at an end. Besides, if the King of the Narrow Way had desired your rescue, He would have stopped you long before now. But since

He has allowed you to proceed so far, it shows that He has no wish for you to turn, but desires your death!"

"Hold! Hold!" exclaimed a stranger, grabbing the arm of Despair – which had just grasped Pilgrim, in order to hurl him into the depths below. "I am sent by King Immanuel!" said he. "I am His minister and messenger to perishing sinners like yourself! Hear, and your soul shall live!"

"The chief of sinners! The chief of sinners!" cried the agonized man – first smiting on his bosom, and then pointing to the pit beneath. "There can be nothing for me except vengeance and fiery indignation, which I see devouring the adversaries of God. What else can I expect, when I have been treasuring up for myself wrath against the day of wrath?"[11]

"While there is life, there is hope!" said the other. "I am an ambassador from the court of Immanuel. I carry with me a treaty of peace! Here are the articles of the treaty," he continued, unfolding the Gospel-Roll, which he carried under his arm. "And now, as an ambassador for Christ, I pray you, in His stead: be reconciled unto God!"[12]

"Alas! Alas!" responded Pilgrim, in plaintive accents. "Your scroll can contain nothing for me but 'lamentation, and mourning, and woe.' I am a sinner to the very uttermost; and my wages are eternal death."

"Listen," said the other, "to what the Lord Immanuel has to say to you!" Now I saw that the messenger opened the roll of parchment, and read to Pilgrim as follows:

"'I HAVE NO PLEASURE IN THE DEATH OF HIM THAT DIETH; BUT RATHER THAT HE WOULD TURN FROM HIS WICKEDNESS, AND LIVE. TURN YE, TURN YE; WHY WILL YE DIE?'[13] 'WHEREFORE HE IS ABLE ALSO TO SAVE THEM TO THE UTTERMOST!'"[14]

---

[11] Romans 2:5.
[12] 2 Corinthians 5:20.
[13] Ezekiel 18:32.
[14] Hebrews 7:25.

"Salvation to the uttermost!" cried the desponding man – the amazing accents sounding like music in his ears! "Can it truly be, that there is still 'forgiveness with God, that he may be feared'?"[15]

"With the Lord," replied the other, "there *is* mercy, and plenteous redemption![16] Indeed, it is of His mercies that you are not consumed; for He might justly have sworn in His wrath, that you should never enter into His rest. But He sends me to bring you back from the gates of death; and to proclaim that it is still 'a faithful saying, and worthy of all acceptation,' that the Lord Immanuel came into the world to save sinners, of whom you are the chief!"[17]

"The chief! The chief indeed!" cried Pilgrim again; "'for mine iniquities have gone over mine head!'[18] They are more than the hairs of my head; therefore, my heart faileth me. Am I not a brand plucked from the burning?"

Despair made one desperate effort to push Pilgrim off the rock, and to plunge him into the pit beneath. But the servant of the Lord Immanuel caught him; and Pilgrim only had enough consciousness remaining to feel the arms of his deliverer thrown around him, and conveying him to a place which he did not know.

---

[15] Psalm 130:4.
[16] Psalm 130:7.
[17] 1 Timothy 1:15.
[18] Psalm 38:4.

Questions for Thought - Chapter One

The young Pilgrim was given advice by his parents as he set out on his journey. What is the Apostle's exhortation to those who are younger? See 1 Peter 5:5. How does Proverbs 13:1 describe the son or daughter who hears the instruction of his/her parents?

Under the influence of Deceiver, Pilgrim found himself being carried along with the crowd of sinners rushing along the Broad Way. How ought he to have combatted the influence of being led down the wrong path? Where can we find strength to stand against the temptation to "go along with the flow" and do something just because "everybody else is doing it"?

In light of the message that the Messenger rushes to bring Pilgrim just as Despair was about to hurl him to everlasting death, what might the Messenger represent? What is represented by the Roll that the Messenger carried? What was the essence of its message?

Entrance into the Narrow-Way-Gate | 2

For a moment, my sleep was broken by these strange visions; but as I renewed my dream, I saw Pilgrim standing before the gate of the Narrow Way, pleading for admission. Above its portals were inscribed, in large characters, these words:

"KNOCK, AND IT SHALL BE OPENED!"

As Pilgrim stood knocking, he observed two men near him, who evidently intended to be the companions of his journey. However, there was something about their manner and appearance which was very unlike what he would have expected from those who were waiting for the opening of the gate. The one, whose name was Procrastination, was lying upon the grass – half-asleep – with his bundle and all of its contents carelessly scattered around him. The other, called Presumption, was seated at the foot of a tree, humming the words of a song. At first, Pilgrim hesitated to address them; but seeing no others with whom he could enter into conversation, he spoke to them thus:

"Good friends, you are intending to be travelers to Zion, I presume?"

"We are," replied the strangers.

"Then," continued Pilgrim, "it is probable that we shall journey together – provided, that is, that you have no objections if I share your company."

"That depends very much upon whether your taste corresponds with ours," said Procrastination, elevating himself. "From our past experience, there are few of the Narrow-Way-travelers who feel inclined to make our acquaintance; and if I may judge from the way in which you were just now knocking at the gate, there is no great likelihood that you will prove to be an exception."

"I suppose we are united," replied Pilgrim, "in our desire to escape as fast as possible from this place of danger, and to get inside the gate."

"True," said Procrastination. "It is my firm purpose to be a Narrow-Way-traveler, and to eventually reach the New Jerusalem. But as yet, I am not inclined to commence the journey. I have not recovered my former fatigues. Before quitting my present resting-place, I must have 'a little more sleep, a little more slumber, a little more folding of the hands to sleep.'"[1]

"I would have you consider well, fellow-traveler," answered Pilgrim (assuming an earnest tone), "whether it is safe to trifle any more of that time away which is soon to come to an end. 'The night is far spent, the day is at hand.'[2] 'He that shall come will come, and will not tarry.'[3] If you resign yourself to slumber now, you may soon sleep the sleep of death! It is surely time – nay, 'it is *high* time to awake out of sleep!'"[4]

Procrastination made no reply. He merely waved his hand and muttered, "Go thy way at this time; at a more convenient season, I will think on these things." He gradually sank down, resumed the position from which he had raised himself, folded his arms, and was steeped in slumber once more.

"You do not need to be under any apprehension of *our* safety," said his companion Presumption, addressing Pilgrim. "We have placed ourselves, as you see, close beside the gate. We are so near to it that we can enter at any time. I shall take care to keep watch for the coming of the Herald of judgment, and there are just a few paces between us and safety."

---

[1] Proverbs 24:33.
[2] Romans 13:12.
[3] Hebrews 10:37.
[4] Romans 13:11.

"Take care," said Pilgrim, "that you do not deceive yourself. You seem to have little idea of your awful and imminent peril. If you wait until the Avenger of blood is in sight – before the key is turned in the lock, He may cut you down! Besides, by presuming upon the patience of the King of the Way; He may leave you to your fate, and 'mock when your fear cometh.'"[5]

"Ah!" replied Presumption. "But I know that Free Grace keeps the keys of the gate, and he never yet was known to reject a traveler that asked for admission."

"Indeed not – to a traveler who seeks entrance there from love to the Lord Immanuel," said Pilgrim. "But to one like yourself, who desires merely to elude the Avenger's sword, and to escape coming wrath – I question whether he would attend to your knockings. Hark!" he continued, as he heard the sound of footsteps from within, approaching the gate. They were accompanied by a voice, exclaiming, "Behold, *now* is the accepted time; behold, *now* is the day of salvation!"[6] The bolts of the gate were drawn aside, and the bars were unloosed. Pilgrim's heart throbbed with joy as he saw the door about to be opened, and he once more urged the two indifferent travelers to cast in their lot with his; but they only repeated their former reply.

Seeing that remonstrance was in vain, Pilgrim eagerly ran up to the gate, exclaiming, "No matter what *others* do – *as for me, I will serve the Lord!*"[7]

"Who stands outside, knocking?" demanded a voice from within.

"A poor traveler," replied Pilgrim, "who received a warrant from the Lord Immanuel, to apply at this gate for admission."

"What is your name?" asked Free Grace, the Keeper of the gate.

"My given name is Sinner," came the answer; "and my surname is Pilgrim."

---

[5] Proverbs 1:26.

[6] 2 Corinthians 6:2.

[7] Joshua 24:15.

"What righteousness do you have?"

"My righteousness," was the reply, "is as filthy rags."[8]

"What plea, then," inquired the Keeper, "do you have to offer?"

"None but this," said Pilgrim; "I am 'wretched, and miserable, and poor, and blind, and naked.'[9] But I have come here to buy gold tried in the fire, that I may be rich; and to obtain white raiment, that I may be clothed; and to have my eyes (which are still scorched with the glare of the pit) anointed with eye-salve, that I may see. Be pleased to open unto me this gate of righteousness,[10] so that I may enter into it and be safe!"

"This way was made," replied the Keeper, "and this gate is opened, just for such sinners as you! Come in, weary and heavy-laden one; and the Lord Immanuel will give you rest."[11] So saying, the gateway turned on its hinges, and disclosed to Pilgrim an aged man with a kind and heavenly expression.

---

[8] Isaiah 66:6.

[9] Revelation 3:17.

[10] Psalm 118:19.

[11] Matthew 11:28.

"For six thousand years," said he, "I have stood at this gate, and been authorized by the Lord of the Way to fling it open to weary travelers; and He is as willing now to welcome them in, as when it was first opened. His love for sinners – the lapse of ages cannot diminish it! Come in, blessed one of the Lord; why do you stand outside?"[12]

Now I saw that the Keeper conducted Pilgrim within the portico of the entrance. Immediately opposite the door of the lodge in which Free Grace dwelt, was a fountain of water. It was surrounded with trees and shrubs that were crowned with greenery of surpassing beauty; and these were reflected, in many hues of loveliness, upon the calm surface. Immediately behind this fountain, rose a temple – upon the pinnacle of which, was a winged cherub, called Gospel, with a trumpet in his hand. With this trumpet, at intervals, he sounded this proclamation: "Ho! every one that thirsteth, come ye to the waters!"[13] And a choir of youthful voices from below, responded: "And the Spirit and the bride say, Come. And let him that heareth say, Come. And let him that is athirst come. And whosoever will, let him take of the water of life freely."[14]

"Can this be the fountain which, a little while ago, I heard celebrated in song by some travelers to Zion?" inquired Pilgrim of Free Grace.

"It is," said the Keeper. "And before you advance farther on your journey, it will be necessary for you to receive a suit of white raiment, washed in its waters."

So saying, he assisted Pilgrim in tearing off the remnants of his ragged covering of self-righteousness. A robe of white linen, which was steeping in the pool – he dried it in the rays of the Sun, and then clothed Pilgrim in it.

Pilgrim stooped over the fountain; and seeing his image reflected in it, he exclaimed in a burst of holy joy, "I will greatly rejoice

---

[12] Genesis 24:31.
[13] Isaiah 55:1.
[14] Revelation 22:17.

in the Lord, my soul shall be joyful in my God; for he hath clothed me with the garments of salvation; he hath covered me with the robe of righteousness!"[15]

Questions for Thought – Chapter Two

Two men were lying around, close to the entrance to the Narrow-Way-Gate; and they were named Procrastination and Presumption. Why were they in such a state of great danger?

Was Pilgrim able to offer anything of his own making at the gate, so that he could be admitted therein? How does Isaiah 66:6 describe those things that we tend to think are good and righteous? What was Pilgrim's only plea for admission?

When Free Grace had brought Pilgrim inside the gate, he gave him a white robe which had been soaking in the fountain of water. What does this represent?

Preparation for the Journey | 3

Now I saw that the Keeper, followed by Pilgrim, entered his dwelling by the side of the gate. They ascended together by a winding staircase, to a turret overlooking the rest of the buildings; and here there was a window that commanded an extensive prospect of the whole Narrow Way. The walls of this chamber were hung with pieces of armor and coats of mail which, from their high polish, shone brilliantly in the morning sun. In the center of the room stood a table with some rolls of parchment lying upon it, and writing materials.

"It is here," said the Keeper, "that travelers receive the whole armor of God, so that they may be able to stand in the evil day. See," continued he, pointing to the walls around him, "how amply the Lord of the Way has provided for the equipment of wayfarers; and truly, this is not too much, considering what is before them."

"What!" exclaimed Pilgrim in astonishment. "I thought that as soon as I was within this gate, those enemies which infest the Broad Way would annoy travelers no longer."

"Ah!" said Free Grace, "you will, before long, discover your mistake. Even he who has been allowed to be the boldest champion that ever trod this way – when he reached the gate of heaven, he was covered with the blood and dust of battle. Oftentimes, in the course of his journey, he was heard to exclaim, 'O wretched man that I am! who shall deliver me from the body of this death?'"[1]

"But who are my enemies, then?" asked Pilgrim. "When they come upon me, I must be prepared to meet them."

---

[1] Romans 7:24.

"That, I cannot tell," answered the Keeper. "Their name is Legion, for they are many. You will not only have to wrestle 'against flesh and blood, but against principalities and powers, against the rulers of the darkness of this world, against spiritual wickedness in high places.'[2] Their tricks and strategies will be numerous. Sometimes they will contend with you in open warfare; sometimes they will try to decoy you from your path; sometimes they will use flattery; sometimes deceit; sometimes threatening. The great adversary – the devil – you may encounter at one time in the form of an angel of light; and at another, as a roaring lion."

"Alas!" exclaimed Pilgrim, greatly alarmed at what he had just heard. "If our foes are thus numerous, which of us can stand? I much fear," said he, with trembling voice, "that I must resign the conflict."

"Yes, truly," said the Keeper, "if you entered this warfare in your own strength; but I should have told you that the great Captain of salvation, Who has been made perfect through suffering, has trodden all the way Himself. He has stopped the mouths of many ravenous lions; quenched with His own blood the violence of many fires; turned to flight the armies of many enemies; through death, He has destroyed him that had the power of death; and He has dragged him in triumph, covered with wounds, at the wheels of His chariot. And now, having thus paved the way, He assures every desponding traveler that if he will only 'put on the whole armour of God, he will be able to stand in the evil day.'" So saying, Free Grace took down – one by one – the pieces of armor which hung upon the walls of the Prospect-Chamber; and he assisted Pilgrim in girding them on. The first piece that he presented to him was a large oval shield of burnished steel. On the front of it was inscribed a selection of Divine promises; and on the inside, carved in larger characters, were these words:

"FEAR NOT, FOR I AM WITH THEE;
BE NOT DISMAYED, FOR I AM THY GOD."

---

[2] Ephesians 6:12.

"This," said Free Grace, "is the Shield of Faith, burnished with the imputed righteousness of the Lord Immanuel. So hard is its metal, that the missiles of the adversary will rebound as they touch it; and they will be able to do you no harm. Here again," continued he, "is another part of your panoply." And he put a massive brass helmet upon Pilgrim's head; its plumes nodded over his brow. "This is called the Helmet of Salvation, wherewith to cover your head in the day of battle. And this," he continued, "is the Breastplate of Righteousness. With it, you will protect your heart – against which, being most vulnerable, the fiery darts of the wicked will frequently be directed."

"And here again," said the Keeper, reaching his hand to a higher part of the wall; "here is a weapon that is *offensive* as well as *defensive*. It is the Sword of the Spirit – without which, the rest of the armor would prove ineffectual." The Keeper drew out the naked weapon from its sheath. It gleamed flashes of light upon the other pieces of armor. "Take this," said he, "in your hand; and never let it go, until you are safe within the walls of the New Jerusalem."

"Would you please fasten the sheath to the girdle which surrounds my waist?" asked Pilgrim.

"No," replied the other. "The sheath must remain with me; never will there be a moment in your journey when that sword can safely be returned to its scabbard, and forsake the hand which grasps it."

"But how, then, can I retain its polish, and keep the rest of the pieces of my armor in their present brightness?" inquired Pilgrim. "If they have no covering or preservative, a few hours' time will corrode them and render them unfit for use."

"You are right," said Free Grace; "and I was about to supply you with what you desire." So I saw that he took a key which was suspended by his side, and opened an ancient oaken cupboard; and from one of its shelves, he brought down a box that was carefully sealed. "Here," said he, "is a box of polish, which you must never omit to use – morning and evening. It is called Prayer; and with it, you will be able to keep 'the whole armour of God' bright and shining. Especially in seasons of peculiar danger and temptation, when the enemy is at hand — be careful to keep rubbing your shield with this polish, in order to preserve its brilliancy, and to not allow the rust to dim its luster or obliterate the promises that are inscribed upon it. These," he continued, "form the principal part of your attire. Here, too, is the golden Girdle of Truth, to fasten around your waist; and to this, I shall presently attach a drinking-cup, by which you may refresh yourself at the fountains in the way. Also, the Sandals of Gospel-peace, which will preserve your feet from the rough and rugged stones scattered in your path. And this — last of all — is the Ring of Adoption!" Free Grace took a richly-polished gem from his jewel-box, and put it upon the same hand with which Pilgrim held the shield. "This," he said, "is the pledge of your sonship; it is the token of your admission into the royal family of heaven, and into the glorious liberty of the sons of God!"

"Behold," exclaimed Pilgrim in adoring wonder, as he listened to the last words which fell from the lips of Free Grace; "behold what manner of love the Father hath bestowed upon me, that *I* should be called the son of God!"[3]

"Yes," replied the other, "it is a glorious privilege; the highest seraph in the Celestial City knows no higher! But remember that although you are a son, you are still a far way off from your heavenly Father's house; and it is fitting for you now to prepare well for the journey before you. But come with me," said Free Grace; "and before you proceed, I shall point out, by means of this large telescope, the country through which your road lies; and I shall also show you the different landmarks which may serve to guide you in safety to Mount Zion." So saying, he opened the window of the turret, which led out to a little balcony. It commanded an extensive view. Lofty mountains in the far distance, on the right and on the left, sparkled in the rays of the midday sun. The rolling slopes of their foothills were studded here and there with towns, villages, and hamlets. The

---

[3] 1 John 3:1.

entire landscape formed one great Valley, which was terminated by the blaze of glory which hid the palaces of Zion from mortal vision. In the midst of this scene, a mountain soared majestically above the rest of the landscape; and Pilgrim observed with his unaided eye, and more distinctly with the telescope, that the Narrow Way led directly up its steep side.

"This valley through which your path lies," said Free Grace, "is still the Valley of Tears – a continuation of the same valley which was the place of your birth, and which is bounded by those bright portals which no human eye has ever penetrated."

Pilgrim endeavored to direct the telescope to the Gate of Heaven. His eyes, however, could not endure the brightness; but from the momentary glance, he caught a view of countless myriads of blessed spirits. They were arrayed in vestures of white; and they had harps in their hands, and crowns upon their heads.

"Who are these arrayed in white robes?" asked Pilgrim. "And whence came they?"[4]

"These are they," answered the other, "who have come out of great tribulation, and have washed their robes, and made them white in the waters of this same fountain; therefore are they now before the throne of God, and serve Him day and night in His temple. They shall hunger no more, neither thirst any more, neither shall the sun light on them, nor any heat; for the Lamb that is in the midst of the throne shall feed them, and shall lead them to living fountains of water; and God shall wipe away all tears from their eyes."

"And," said Pilgrim, still looking through the telescope, "I think I see, gathered upon the turrets of the golden palaces, crowds of spectators – their eyes directed upon this Valley of Tears, watching the travelers as they journey towards Zion!"

"These," replied Free Grace, "are the redeemed from the earth – the patriarchs, saints, and prophets of former generations; who, 'through faith and patience, are now inheriting the promises.' Their

---

[4] Revelation 7:13, 17.

warfare is accomplished, but they still delight to follow the travelers they have left behind. 'Wherefore, seeing thou also art compassed about with so great a cloud of witnesses, lay aside every weight, and the sin that doth more easily beset thee, and run with patience the race that is set before thee.'"[5]

"Then, from what you are saying," said Pilgrim, laying aside the telescope, "I may feel the assurance that since I am now safe within this gate, God's covenant-love shall never be taken from me!"

"Do you see yonder colossal barriers?" asked the Keeper, pointing to the distant mountains. Their tops rested amidst the clouds, as if they were the emblems of immutability. "The King of the Way Himself has declared that sooner shall these mountains depart, and these hills be removed; than that His love should be taken from you, or the covenant of His peace be removed."[6]

"Blessed thought!" exclaimed Pilgrim. "Surely it is enough to dispel every fear. But what else of the way?"

"I will not detain you," said Free Grace. "After leaving this gate, continue to follow the strait and narrow path, without deviating to the right hand or to the left. Do not forsake it because it becomes too narrow, or because it assumes the aspect of a dreary wilderness. Was it not this which tempted you at first to stray down the Broad Road – the fact that there was no apparent beauty nor comeliness in the Narrow Way to make it desirable?"

"True," replied Pilgrim. "I shall faithfully follow your directions."

"Well," continued the other, "follow this narrow path until it brings you to the Mount of Ordinances. There you will find a lodging-place, prepared by the Lord of the Way for the rest and refreshment of travelers; and there you will receive further directions for proceeding upon your journey."

Upon returning to the Prospect-Chamber, the Keeper took one of the rolls of parchment which lay upon the table; and folding it up

---

[5] Hebrews 12:1.
[6] Isaiah 54:10.

carefully, he requested Pilgrim to deposit it close to his heart, underneath his breastplate. "This," said he, "is your Passport and Charter – written with blood that was shed by Immanuel, the Son of the Highest. This Passport will be demanded of you at the Gate of Heaven; and without it, entrance cannot be obtained. There are many like yourself, who wish to arrive at the Celestial City by a shortcut from the Broad Road; so they try to avoid the Narrow-Way-Gate by climbing over the wall. But since they have no Passport when they arrive at the portals of Mount Zion, their plea is rejected; and all the toil of their pilgrimage goes for nothing."

Pilgrim unfolded this Charter which contained his spiritual privileges, and he found it to contain these amazing words:

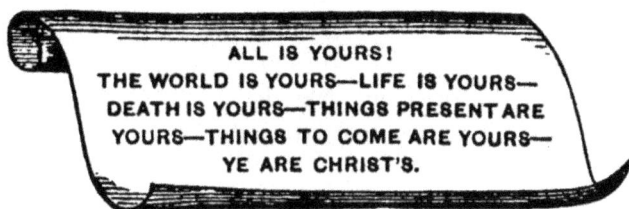

> **ALL IS YOURS!**
> **THE WORLD IS YOURS—LIFE IS YOURS—**
> **DEATH IS YOURS—THINGS PRESENT ARE**
> **YOURS—THINGS TO COME ARE YOURS—**
> **YE ARE CHRIST'S.**

Being now fully equipped and ready for his journey, Pilgrim and Free Grace descended the stairs which led from the armory. Pilgrim was just about to bid Free Grace farewell, when the latter said: "Hark! Do you hear that distant music?"

Pilgrim listened, and a melodious sound came floating to his ear; but it wafted from such a distance as to be scarcely audible.

"What anthem of triumph is that?" inquired Pilgrim.

"It is the joy in heaven over another returning sinner!" replied Free Grace. "When the heavenly Watchmen, who crowd the battlements of Zion, first caught a glimpse of your burnished armor – that was the signal for that burst of jubilee. Your entrance within the Narrow-Way-Gate will not allow one harp there to be silent this day!"

Pilgrim felt greatly strengthened by such a thought; and Free Grace – once more pressing his hand – committed him to the keeping of the King of the Way.

"The Lord be with you," said Free Grace, still keeping his arms extended as he pronounced his benediction upon the departing traveler. "The Lord be with you, and keep you. The Lord cause His face to shine upon you; the Lord give you peace.[7] The Lord be thy stay on thy right hand; the Lord suffer not the sun to smite you by day, nor the moon by night."[8]

Then Pilgrim went on his way rejoicing, and saying, "The Lord is on my side; I will not fear what man shall do unto me! The Lord is my Shepherd; I shall not want. The Lord is my light and my salvation; whom shall I fear? The Lord is the strength of my life; of whom shall I be afraid? Who shall separate me from the love of Christ? Shall tribulation, or distress, or persecution, or famine, or nakedness, or peril, or sword? Nay! In all these things, I shall be more than conqueror![9] Thanks be to God, Who giveth me the victory!"

---

[7] Numbers 6:24-26.

[8] Psalm 121:5-8.

[9] Romans 8:35-37.

Questions for Thought – Chapter Three

Free Grace took Pilgrim into a room full of armor with which to outfit the travelers in the King's Way. What was Pilgrim's reaction when the Keeper indicated that this armor was a necessity for his journey, and why did he react that way? Why couldn't the Keeper tell Pilgrim who his enemies were? Who or what are some of the spiritual enemies that you face on a daily basis?

Why did the Keeper keep the sheath for the sword with himself, instead of allowing Pilgrim to use it to carry his sword on his waist?

The pieces of the armor of God are detailed by the Apostle Paul in Ephesians 6, but there is one thing that is generally left out when the pieces of armor are spoken of. However, Mr. MacDuff has done well to include it in the ensemble with which Free Grace outfitted Pilgrim. The Keeper took this object out of the ancient cupboard, after he had refused to give the sword-sheath to Pilgrim. What was it, and what was its vital purpose?

In the Valley with Backslider | 4

Now I saw in my dream that, in obedience to the injunctions of the Keeper of the Gate, Pilgrim went on his journey. Lofty trees spread their foliage over his head; brooks of water flowed at his side; and here and there, flowers (said to be transplanted from the gardens of the Celestial City, by the Lord of the Way Himself) filled the air with their fragrance.

As Pilgrim proceeded, however, the aspect of the road began to change; the path which he had hitherto been following became less defined. Sometimes it lay through a narrow ravine; sometimes through marshy ground, or intersected with torrents of water; sometimes it led up steep places – in the ascent of which, had it not been for the sandals with which Free Grace had provided him, he would have slipped frequently. At times, he was even tempted to forget the strict directions that he had received, which had forbidden him to deviate from the straight road on account of its ruggedness. But whenever he did so, he had abundant reason for regret. I saw, indeed, on one occasion, that – while following a forbidden path – he stumbled and lost one of his sandals. The shock made him fall with violence to the ground, and his shield rolled into the mud. But forthwith, he opened his box of polish to restore its brightness. This he did upon his bended knees, confessing that "he stumbled, being disobedient." And he entreated the Lord of the Way to show him the path wherein he should walk, and to "lead him in the way everlasting."[1]

I observed that after Pilgrim had advanced a considerable way, he was walking through a secluded valley at nightfall. As he paused

---

[1] Psalm 139:24.

for a moment to enjoy the quiet scene, his ear was arrested by plaintive cries which came from no great distance from the path. They were tones of deep distress. He listened again; and he heard moanings that sounded as if they came from a dying man, accompanied with bitter lamentations. Pilgrim, having a sympathetic heart, forthwith proceeded to the spot whence the melancholy sounds were heard. He had not advanced many steps before discovering an individual, whose similarity of dress revealed him to be a fellow-traveler. He lay covered with dust, blood trickled from a wound in his side, his sword was flung away from him, and he was uttering doleful shrieks and cries. Pilgrim could only gather up the reason for his lamentation in the intervals between his sobs, and the man seemed unconscious of his presence for a long time. "Oh!" exclaimed the melancholy sufferer, as he wrung his hands in agony. "Oh that it were with me as in months past, when his candle shined upon my head; and when, by his light, I walked through darkness!"[2]

"Alas! Poor man," said Pilgrim, coming up and trying to comfort him. "What is the cause of your deep dejection?"

The stranger made no reply; but he continued to groan more bitterly, and to cry more loudly, "The Lord hath forgotten to be gracious, and his tender mercies are clean gone for ever."[3]

"What is your name?" asked Pilgrim again, with a tear of heartfelt sympathy rolling down his own cheek.

"My name is Backslider," said the other, startled by the unexpected feeling that was being shown to him; "and rightly have I been so called."

"How did you come to lie here in this bed of dust?" inquired Pilgrim. "Where is your shield?"

"I have thrown it away," replied Backslider, "because it is of no more use to me. You will find it yonder," continued he – pointing to a place covered with mud, a few yards from his side.

Pilgrim lifted up a plate of rusted metal, which he never could have recognized to be a shield – although it had once been as brilliant and shiny as that which he had in his own hand. The promises that were inscribed on it were either entirely effaced, or so covered with rust as to be illegible.

As Pilgrim returned the shield to its former owner, he asked, "Why did you throw away a weapon so necessary for your safety, and allow it to become thus corroded with rust? Did not Free Grace supply you at the Narrow-Way-Gate with Prayer-polish, in order to keep your whole coat of armor bright?"

"He did! He did!" exclaimed the agonized man – the recollection of the fact extracting an even deeper sigh from his heart. "But last night, after I had climbed the steep rock that you must have ascended a little while ago, I felt so fatigued that I lay down to sleep – omitting to polish my armor. And when I awoke in the morning,

---

[2] Job 29:2.
[3] Psalm 77:9.

not only had the rust begun to cover it, but lo! – upon examining my traveler's bag, I found that the box of polish had dropped out during the night, and had rolled down to the bottom of the precipice."

"But did you not return to recover it?" inquired Pilgrim.

"No," said Backslider. "I felt greatly disinclined to descend the rock. Besides, there is close by me here a bed of sand, with which I tried to remove the rust; and it seemed to answer the purpose so well, that I thought I could get along without my lost polish."

"Foolish traveler! – to forget so soon the injunctions of the Porter at the Gate," said Pilgrim. "But why do you not return and recover the polish without delay?"

"Alas!" replied he, in a tone of deep despondency. "I cannot! I am so weak from the loss of blood, that I am utterly unable to rise."

"How did you receive that wound?" inquired Pilgrim.

"In an unguarded moment," said Backslider, "when I ventured to lay my armor aside, an adversary called Besetting Sin took a deadly aim; a poisoned arrow sped from his bow, and pierced my heart. For many hours, I have been lying here – stretched upon this couch of tears and blood, listening to nothing but the echo of my own piteous cries, and unable to go even the short distance to that little brook to moisten my parched tongue. Had the King of the Way been intending to save me," he continued, "He would have given me help long before this; but 'my way is surely hid from the Lord, and my judgment is passed over from my God.'[4] He is weary of me, and rightly so; and He leaves me to perish."

"Nay, nay, poor sufferer!" replied Pilgrim. "'Hast thou not known, hast thou not heard, that the everlasting God, the Lord, the Creator of the ends of the earth, fainteth not, neither is weary? Even the youths shall faint, and be weary, and the young men shall utterly fall; but they that wait upon the Lord shall renew their strength.'[5]

---

[4] Isaiah 40:27.

[5] Isaiah 40:28, 30, 31.

'Wait on the Lord, then; be of good courage, and he shall strengthen thine heart. Wait, I say, on the Lord!'"[6]

Now I saw that Pilgrim ran and filled the silver drinking-cup which had been given him at the gate, with the water of the adjoining brook. He put it to the man's pale lips. He had no sooner tasted the refreshing water, than a glow of new life radiated from his countenance. His sunken eyes revived, and were lighted up with returning animation.

For the first time, the sufferer spoke in a tone of calm composure, with tears – not of sorrow, but of gratitude – starting to his eyes. "Whosoever giveth a cup of cold water to a fainting disciple, he shall not lose his reward,"[7] said Backslider.

Pilgrim bathed the sufferer's brow with the cooling water. He washed his wound, and staunched it by applying some fresh linen which had been given him by the Keeper of the Gate. He also opened his traveler's bag, and shared a part of the Bread of Life with the reviving man. Producing his own box of Prayer-polish, they united together in endeavoring to restore the corroded shield to its former brightness. Having assisted him in buckling on his armor, and shaking off the remaining dust which adhered to it – Pilgrim conducted him, once more, to the Narrow Way from which he had wandered. Here they separated – Backslider to return and recover his lost polish; and Pilgrim to pursue, without delay, his journey Zionward.

---

[6] Psalm 27:14.
[7] Matthew 10:42.

Questions for Thought - Chapter Four

Pilgrim found a man named Backslider in the valley through which he was traveling — wounded, defenseless, and sorrowful. What was the condition of Backslider's shield, and how did it get that way?

When responding to the backslider, Pilgrim did not wag his finger of judgment at him; rather, he lovingly listened to him, and comforted him with promises from the Scriptures. Then he helped him restore the shine of his rusty shield with some of his own prayer-polish. How important do you think a true Christian friend is to someone who is backsliding, and why? Check out James 5:20.

In Psalm 73, the Psalmist was considering backsliding himself, when he saw the worldly prosperity of wicked unbelievers. But there is a pivotal point in that Psalm (verses 16, 17) when he did something that changed his perspective. "When I thought to know this, it was too painful for me; Until I went into the sanctuary of God; then understood I their end." Why might attending public worship regularly be such a help against the sin of backsliding?

At the Palace of the Royal Psalmist | 5

Now I saw in my dream that Pilgrim had entered a richer and more fertile country. The mountains and valleys which he had been traversing for some time – many of which were bleak and bare – were now exchanged for a region that was waving with crops of great luxuriance, and which was sometimes alternated with verdant meadows and wooded slopes. Pilgrim arrived at a place that was shadowed, on either side, with trees of enormous size. Their leafy tops formed a noble archway over his head, and the walls which rose on either side suggested that he was in the neighborhood of some princely residence. He had not advanced much farther when he observed that the road was terminated by a gateway, which was surmounted with the arms of royalty. The gate was wide open for the free passage of travelers; and upon inquiring at the gatehouse about the owner of the residence, Pilgrim was informed that this was the Palace of the Royal Psalmist of Israel – who had made provision in his regal mansion for the comfort and refreshment of wayfarers to Zion.

Pilgrim had now been without sleep for some days, and he rejoiced at the prospect of approaching rest. As he walked along the avenue which led to the Palace, his ear caught melodious sounds proceeding from the interior of the building. He stood for many minutes, with delighted fascination, as he listened to the morning prayer of praise – in which timbrel, lute, harp, and organ seemed to have combined their richest harmonies in summoning all nature to rise and do homage to its Maker.

Praise ye the Lord!
Praise ye the Lord from the heavens. Praise him in the heights.
Praise ye him, all his angels. Praise ye him, all his hosts.

The Great Journey

Praise ye him, sun and moon. Praise him, all ye stars of light.
Praise him, ye heavens of heavens, and ye waters that be
above the heavens.
Let them praise the name of the Lord; for he commanded,
and they were created.
He hath also stablished them for ever and ever; he hath made a decree
which shall not pass.
Praise the Lord from the earth, ye dragons and all deeps;
Fire and hail, snow and vapours, stormy wind fulfilling his word;
Mountains and all hills; fruitful trees and all cedars;
Beasts and all cattle; creeping things and flying fowl;
Kings of the earth and all people; princes and all judges of the earth:
Both young men and maidens; old men and children:
Let them praise the name of the Lord,
For his name alone is excellent; his glory is above the earth and heaven.
He also exalteth the horn of his people, the praise of all his saints;
Even of the children of Israel, a people near unto him.
Praise ye the Lord![1]

When the cadence of this anthem had died away, Pilgrim approached the door; and after knocking, a servant of the Palace welcomed him in. Upon entering, he found himself in the center of a great hall; which was built of the choicest timber from the cedar-forests of Lebanon, with the trophies of battle hung all around the walls. On one side were many gleaming coats of mail, which had been taken as spoil from the giants of Philistia – several of which measured nine feet in length. On the other side, Pilgrim beheld the tawny hide of a lion, with the fleece of a little lamb by its side – the memorials of a hard-won encounter with this monarch of the forest. Over an enormous javelin – with a staff that was like a weaver's beam – a few stones hung suspended in a sling; and they told the story of a bloody encounter, in which the prowess of a daring champion had been humbled by a few pebbles from the brook.

After gazing upon these things, Pilgrim was conducted by the servant to the hall from which the music had proceeded –

---

[1] Psalm 148.

which was still rolling on in solemn grandeur. When Pilgrim entered, he beheld an aged monarch. His head was silvered with years; he was seated upon a golden throne, and he had a harp in his hand. Around him were collected groups of singers and choristers, performing upon different instruments.

The Royal Psalmist cast a glance at the visitor; but without interrupting the sacred song, he beckoned to him to come and join their chorus: "'O magnify the Lord with me, and let us exalt his name together!'[2] 'Come, ye that fear the Lord, and tell what he hath done for your soul!'"[3]

"'I sought the Lord,'" said Pilgrim, unable to keep silence any longer. "'He heard me, and delivered me from all my fears.'[4] 'He brought me up also out of an horrible pit, and out of the miry clay, and set my feet upon a rock, and established my goings.'"[5]

The Psalmist converted this into a new theme of thanksgiving, and again he awoke his harp-strings: "This poor man cried, and the Lord heard him, and saved him out of all his troubles. O fear the Lord, ye his saints; for there is no want to them that fear him. The young lions do lack and suffer hunger; but they that wait on the Lord shall not lack any good thing."[6] And then, turning to the bands of youthful choristers below, he continued his song. "Come, ye children, hearken unto me, and I will teach you the fear of the Lord. What man is he that desireth life, and loveth many days, that he may see good? Keep thy tongue from evil, and thy lips from speaking guile; depart from evil, and do good. Seek peace, and pursue it."[7]

Sometimes a more plaintive chord was struck; and the recollection of by-gone transgression, coming before the mind of the aged monarch, would draw a tear to his eye. At other times, not himself,

[2] Psalm 34:3.
[3] Psalm 66:19.
[4] Psalm 34:4.
[5] Psalm 40:2.
[6] Psalm 34:6, 9, 10.
[7] Psalm 34:11-14.

but the triumphs of the King of the Way formed the theme of his song. "Thou hast ascended on high. Thou hast led captivity captive. Thou hast received gifts for men; yea, for the rebellious also, that the Lord God might dwell among them."[8] At still other times, the Psalmist's eye would glow with prophetic fire; and he would make the chords tell of the glories of that future time yet to come – when, instead of a few solitary travelers, the Narrow Way would be crowded with Pilgrims to Zion; and the Lord Immanuel would be exalted upon the throne of universal empire. "He shall have dominion also from sea to sea, and from the river to the ends of the earth. They that dwell in the wilderness shall bow before him, and his enemies shall lick the dust. The kings of Tarshish, and of the isles, shall bring presents. The kings of Seba and Sheba shall offer gifts. His name shall endure for ever. It shall be continued as long as the sun, and men shall be blessed in him. All nations shall call him blessed!"

When these majestic notes had died away, Pilgrim was conducted by his attendant to a chamber in the Palace. There, the servant had prepared water for him to wash his feet, and also to refresh himself.

"How often," inquired Pilgrim, "does your Royal Master engage in these exercises of devotion?"

"Seven times a day does he praise God, because of His righteous judgments.[9] Often does he 'meditate upon him in the night-watches'; and at midnight," continued the servant, "he arises to give thanks to Him for His mercies!"[10]

Upon Pilgrim's return to the banquet-hall, he shared with the aged king "a feast of fat things, a feast of wines on the lees; of fat things full of marrow, of wines on the lees well refined." Besides these things, there was also a plate of heavenly manna, which had been gathered in the pleasure-grounds of the Palace; a jar full of pure water from the Fountain of Salvation; and honey from the rocky

---

[8] Psalm 68:18.
[9] Psalm 119:164.
[10] Psalm 63:6.

sides of Mount Pisgah, which rose in full view from the window. When the banquet was finished, the Monarch poured some of the living water into the cup of salvation, saying, "Let us take the cup of salvation, and call upon the name of the Lord. Let us now pay our vows together, in the presence of His people."[11]

Then I saw that the guest and his entertainer continued sitting together, encouraging one another with conversation about the Lord of the Way, and about the glories that were awaiting His travelers. "What shall we render!" exclaimed Pilgrim, bursting into an exclamation of holy gratitude for the rich provision which had been set before him. "What shall we render unto God for all his benefits towards us?[12] 'Bless the Lord, O my soul; and all that is within me, bless his holy name!'"[13]

"I will sing," exclaimed the other, "unto the Lord as long as I live! I will sing praises unto my God while I have any being.[14] Oh! How great is his goodness, which he has laid up for them that fear him; which he has wrought for them that trust in him before the sons of men!"[15]

Pilgrim continued – again detailing the wonders that God had done for him. "'The sorrows of death compassed me, and the pains of hell gat hold upon me: I found trouble and sorrow. Then I called upon the name of the Lord. O Lord! I beseech thee, deliver my soul!'[16] 'He 'delivered my soul from death,' mine eyes from tears, and 'my feet from falling';[17] and he hath now set me in 'a large place,' and 'delivered me, because he delighted in me.'[18] He hath fed me also with 'the finest of the wheat: and with honey out of the

---

[11] Psalm 116:13.
[12] Psalm 116:12.
[13] Psalm 103:1.
[14] Psalm 146:2.
[15] Psalm 31:19.
[16] Psalm 116:3, 4.
[17] Psalm 56:13.
[18] Psalm 18:19.

rock' hath he satisfied me.[1] 'O that men would praise the Lord for his goodness, and for his wonderful works unto the children of men!'"[2]

"'I have been young,'" responded the aged monarch – detailing, in his turn, the experience of an eventful life – "'I have been young, and now am old; yet I have never seen the righteous forsaken, nor his seed begging bread.'[3] 'Happy is he who hath the God of Jacob for his help: whose hope is in the Lord his God!'"[4]

With such themes of conversation, the Psalmist of Israel and the traveler to Zion entertained themselves at the close of the day. Night was beginning to close around them. Rock, forest, and mountain – which spread before them in the extensive view from the window of the banquet-chamber – began to be enveloped in a sable covering. Soon afterwards, the sky was bespangled with stars; and the silvery moon rose behind the summit of Mount Pisgah. The Psalmist, with his harp in his hand, conducted Pilgrim out to a large balcony in front of the window. The harp-strings were once more awakened; and amidst the stillness of the night, the air was again vocal with praise.

"'The heavens,'" commenced the aged king – joining his voice with the music – "'the heavens declare the glory of God; and the firmament sheweth forth his handiwork. Day unto day uttereth speech, and night unto night sheweth knowledge.'[5] 'When I consider thy heavens, the work of thy fingers, the moon and the stars, which thou hast ordained; what is man, that thou art mindful of him? and the son of man, that thou visitest him?'"[6]

Their evening song being ended, Pilgrim was again conducted to his sleeping apartment, where he mused in gratitude upon all of

---

[1] Psalm 81:16.
[2] Psalm 107:31.
[3] Psalm 37:25.
[4] Psalm 146:5.
[5] Psalm 19:1, 2.
[6] Psalm 8:3, 4.

the goodness and mercy which had been made to pass before him. And then, having imparted a brighter than ordinary polish to his armor, he cast himself upon his bed and closed his eyes in slumber. His sleep was crowded with dreams of the preceding day; and he continued to enjoy his soothing rest, undisturbed, until an early hour in the morning, when the soft cadence of the harp stole upon his ear once more. Raising himself from his pillow, he listened. It was the aged monarch, who had already begun his morning praises. These words reached Pilgrim's ears: "'My voice shalt thou hear in the morning, O Lord! in the morning will I direct my prayer unto thee, and will look up.'[7] 'I laid me down and slept; I awaked: for the Lord sustained me!'[8] 'My soul waiteth for the Lord, more than they that watch for the morning. I say, more than they that do watch for the morning!'[9] 'When I awake, I am still with thee!'"[10]

Pilgrim could have joyfully tarried many days upon this spot of holy ground, but he saw that it would be necessary for him to continue his journey. Therefore, he resolved to set out without delay, in hopes that the morning's dawn would find him upon the summit of Mount Pisgah – across which, his pathway led; and from whence, he would obtain a nearer glimpse of the Land of Promise and the Celestial City. Accordingly, having girded on his armor again, he bade his royal Entertainer an affectionate farewell. The aged Psalmist once more embraced his guest, and – committing him to the keeping of the King of the Way – invoked on his harp a benediction upon his departure: "The Lord hear thee in the day of trouble; the name of the God of Jacob defend thee; send thee help from the sanctuary, and strengthen thee out of Zion; remember all thy offerings, and accept thy burnt sacrifice; grant thee according to thine own heart, and fulfil all thy counsel."[11]

---

[7] Psalm 5:3.
[8] Psalm 3:5.
[9] Psalm 130:6.
[10] Psalm 139:18.
[11] Psalm 20:1-4.

John Ross MacDuff

Pilgrim proceeded on his journey, until the last faint sounds of the melody died away on the morning breeze. Soon he was once more outside the gate, in the depths of the forest; but, being full of faith and hope, "he went on his way rejoicing."

Questions for Thought - Chapter Five

When we are tired and weary on our life's pilgrimage, our focus often shifts towards ourselves, our problems, and our difficulties. But the Royal Singer's songs were not centered upon himself. Who was the general subject of attention in his songs?

The great Reformer Martin Luther once said, "[The Psalms are] a little Bible, wherein everything contained in the entire Bible is beautifully and briefly comprehended." The great under-arching theme of the whole Bible is the good news of the Gospel of redemption by Jesus Christ. When you are tired and weary, do you find that the Book of Psalms helps to direct your focus upon the One Who can give true rest?

In addition to the reading and memorizing of the Psalms, what is another way that we might incorporate the Psalms into our everyday Christian life? See Ephesians 5:19, 20 and Colossians 3:16, 17.

Through the Furnace of Affliction | 6

Now I saw in my dream that Pilgrim continued to pursue his path, unobstructed, for many days. His heart was filled with "all peace and joy in believing." His way led through a rich, rolling countryside, where quiet rivers wound their way through wooded knolls and lush meadows. Here and there, shepherds and their flocks were reposing upon the meadows, or seeking shelter from the sultry heat amidst the thickets which fringed the edges of the streams. At times, Pilgrim delighted to enter into conversation with them; and they often sang together words with which he had become familiar in the Palace of the sweet Psalmist of Israel: "The Lord is my Shepherd, I shall not want. He maketh me to lie down in green pastures: he leadeth me beside the still waters. He restoreth my soul: he leadeth me in the paths of righteousness for his own name's sake."[1]

But although Pilgrim was now enjoying these periods of spiritual refreshment, he was soon to be reminded of the great truth which the Keeper of the Gate had forewarned him of – that the pathway to the Celestial City is one of "much tribulation."[2]

After advancing some days upon his journey, Pilgrim beheld in the distance – in the very center of the Narrow Way – a large fire, resembling a blazing furnace. It was called "the Furnace of Affliction." Upon reaching it, he trembled with fear; his knees smote one against the other; the Shield of Faith fell, with its face to the earth; and he wrung his hands in despair. As he stood with his eyes fastened upon the ground, they happened to glance on the inside of his shield – upon which, he read this inscription:

---

[1] Psalm 23:1-3.
[2] Revelation 7:14.

"FEAR NOT, FOR I AM WITH THEE; BE NOT DISMAYED,
FOR I AM THY GOD. WHEN THOU PASSEST THROUGH THE FIRE,
THOU SHALT NOT BE BURNED."[3]

After reading this promise of the Lord of the Way, Pilgrim tried to resume his courage; and he made an effort to lift up the weapon which, from its fall, was covered with the mire of the road. But again, his hand fell powerless; and he himself sunk to the earth! Now as he thus lay fainting under the heat of the fire – terrified at the thought of being obliged to pass through its flames – a person was seen approaching. It was a woman clothed in a black robe, with a meek expression upon her countenance. Her name was Resignation. She approached with slow and silent steps, and addressed Pilgrim thus:

"Think it not strange, afflicted traveler, concerning this fiery trial that is to try you, as if some strange thing happened unto you; but rather, rejoice!"[4]

"How can I rejoice," asked Pilgrim – his voice quivering as he spoke – "when I must plunge into tormenting flames?"

"Nay, nay," replied Resignation. "You should have known that the Lord Immanuel – whose nature and whose name is Love – would never have placed anything upon the way which would destroy those whom He has bought with His own blood."

"Is not the purpose of fire," asked Pilgrim, "to destroy?"

"Yes," replied the other, "there *are* fires for destruction; but there are fires for *purification* also. The flames in the bottomless pit, which you once saw, *are* flames to consume. But these," she continued, pointing to the furnace before her, "are flames to *refine*. And the light sufferings that they inflict, which are 'but for a moment,' will work out for you 'a far more exceeding and eternal weight of glory.'"[5]

---

[3] Isaiah 43:1, 2.
[4] 1 Peter 4:12.
[5] 2 Corinthians 4:17.

"But," said Pilgrim, "I have no strength of my own for passing through this awful furnace!"

"Fear not!" replied Resignation. "The Lord of the Way has promised to make His strength perfect in weakness. In fact," said she, pointing to the center of the flames, "can you not see, in the midst of that burning fiery furnace, 'one like unto the Son of God'? Immanuel Himself was made perfect through a furnace of suffering – far more scorching than this; and He waits to conduct you through! Only be strong, and of a good courage; gird on your armor, walk boldly forward, and not a hair of your head shall be singed."

"But," continued Pilgrim, his faith still wavering, "is there no by-road which the King has provided, by which travelers may avoid this great and unnecessary evil?"

"Call it not 'unnecessary,' faithless one," said Resignation. "If you had not – in your fear – thrown down your shield into the mud of the road, you would have read one of the most comforting of all of the promises inscribed there: 'I afflict not willingly, nor grieve the children of men.'[6] That fiery furnace would never have been there, if it *could* have been spared."

So saying, Resignation lifted up the shield from the mud. She asked Pilgrim for the Prayer-polish to restore its brightness, and to make visible the many obliterated promises which covered its face. He sprung up from his posture of weakness, and once more stood ready in his armor. "It is deep ingratitude in me," said he, addressing Resignation, "to thus distrust the Lord of the Way, when I remember what great things He hath done for me in times past. And now, therefore, I shall resolutely 'go in the strength of the Lord God!'[7] 'Though he slay me, yet will I trust in him!'"[8]

Now I saw that Pilgrim immediately rushed into the midst of the furnace, and Resignation followed him. He uttered a few cries from the smartings of the flames; but He Whose form he had seen in the midst of the fires, supported him with His arm. He divided the flames before him, and whispered words of peace into his ear. He gave him some ointment, called "Grace," to enable him to bear the pain; and He put a bracelet upon his arm, as another pledge of adoption – upon which, Pilgrim afterwards found this inscription:

"WHOM THE LORD LOVETH, HE CHASTENETH."

Moreover, with a censer full of much incense (which He held in His hand), He perfumed Pilgrim's person and gave a perpetual efficacy to the Prayer-polish. Then He pointed him upwards to the top of the Mount of Ordinances, saying: "There I will meet with you and commune with you from the Mercy-seat." After that, He vanished out of Pilgrim's sight.

---

[6] Lamentations 3:33.
[7] Psalm 71:16.
[8] Job 13:15.

No sooner had Pilgrim come forth from the furnace, than he broke out into a song of triumphant joy. "'It was good for me that I was afflicted!'[9] God has been 'my refuge and strength, a very present help in trouble.'[10] 'Thou hast upholden me by thy right hand.'[11] 'When I said, My foot slippeth; thy mercy, O Lord, held me up.'[12] 'Heart and flesh faileth; but God is the strength of my heart, and my portion for ever!'"[13]

As Pilgrim looked upon his armor, it shone with a greater luster. The plumes of his helmet, which had lost their original hues by being covered with the dust of the way, were purified. His sword, which had been made dim by long exposure, gleamed with fresh brilliancy. The rust that had been contracted in the plates of his armor, was removed by the flames. He himself had acquired fresh ardor for his journey; and for a long time afterwards, his memory continued to cherish the furnace as a place of "reviving and refreshing from the presence of the Lord."[14]

[9] Psalm 119:71.
[10] Psalm 46:1.
[11] Psalm 73:23.
[12] Psalm 94:18.
[13] Psalm 73:26.
[14] Acts 3:19.

Questions for Thought - Chapter Six

Pilgrim was at a point where he was enjoying periods of spiritual refreshment, but he soon met with something that he had been forewarned of by the Keeper of the Gate. Why is it unwise for us to expect to travel to the Celestial City without encountering difficulties and afflictions? See Revelation 7:14. How do we know that these afflictions are absolutely necessary for us to endure? See Lamentations 3:33.

Why is affliction good for pilgrims on their way to the heavenly City? Pilgrim was afraid to pass through the furnace because he knew that the work of fire is destruction, until Resignation showed him the other purpose of fire. What is the difference between the fires of hell, from which the Lord has redeemed us; and the fires of affliction, which He calls us to pass through?

Whom did Resignation point Pilgrim's eyes to, in the midst of the flames? Afflictions not only cause us to see just how helpless we are in ourselves, but they also show us our utter dependence upon the Lord. How does it change your outlook on the subject of afflictions, when you realize that Son of God was made perfect through a fiery furnace of suffering? Does it comfort you to know that He Himself is there to conduct us through the fires which we are to pass through?

On the Mount of Ordinances | 7

It was now evening, and Pilgrim was approaching the base of Mount Pisgah. The full moon had again risen over its rocky steeps; and it vied with the fires which he had just left behind him, in lighting up his path. Before Resignation had parted from him, she had directed him on the way. And although the mountain was lofty and very steep, he felt such enlargement of heart that, before long, he found himself in safety upon the summit. The pale moon-beams just shed sufficient light to conduct him to a cavern that was hollowed out in the rock, where a natural bed was formed. Upon this, Pilgrim flung himself down to rest – covering himself carefully with his shield. And in a few minutes, his eyes were closed in slumber – but not without a longing expectation of the prospect that was awaiting him on the approaching morning.

Now I saw in my dream that when the morning began to break, Pilgrim rose from his bed; and after carefully polishing his armor, and buckling it on, he came out of the cavern which had formed his resting-place for the night. The sun was pouring a flood of light upon the valley at his feet, which was terminated in the far distance by the glittering palaces of Mount Zion.

Behind him lay the long road which he had lately traversed, with its varying landscape of both forests and mountains. When he thought of the way by which the Lord had led him – of the difficulties that he had overcome, the enemies that he had vanquished, and the seasons of refreshment which he had enjoyed – he could not refrain from following the example of other travelers, by setting up a stone of remembrance at the mouth of the cavern, with this inscription upon it:

The Great Journey

"HITHERTO HATH THE LORD HELPED ME!"[1]

Never before, during the course of his journey, did Pilgrim feel such enlargement as he did here! The previous night of weeping and affliction had been well-worth enduring, on account of the joy that now came in the morning! The pure atmosphere which he breathed — far above the mists which overhung the path below — gave him a buoyancy of spirit, to which he had been a stranger up until now. Nor could he forget the fact that he owed much of this holy joy to the refining furnace — through which he had so lately passed, and which (at the time) had appeared so terrible.

Now I saw that Pilgrim approached an eminent place, which — being immediately adjoining — often gave its name to the entire mountain. It was called the Mount of Ordinances. Here he found an arbor erected for the refreshment of travelers. It was hollowed out of the living rock; and it was blooming with flowers of much loveliness, which the King of the Way had transplanted from the gardens of the Celestial City. Upon a little table in the center of the arbor, was placed some bread and wine. Of these, travelers were invited to partake — as memorials of the King's dying love, as well as for the nourishment of their own souls.

These words were chiseled upon the rock, above the entrance:

"DO THIS IN REMEMBRANCE OF ME!"[2]

And when Pilgrim had entered, he found himself welcomed by a servant of the Lord Immanuel, with the Gospel-Roll in his hand.

"Welcome," said the servant, "to this gracious feast that the Lord of the Way hath provided for you! 'Eat, drink! Yea, drink abundantly, O beloved!'"[3]

Pilgrim gladly partook of the gracious provision. "Surely," he exclaimed, as he broke the heavenly manna in his hands — "surely

---

[1] 1 Samuel 7:12.
[2] Luke 22:19.
[3] Song of Solomon 5:1.

the Lord is in this place, and I knew it not; this is none other than the house of God; this is the very gate of heaven!"[4]

"The Great Captain of your salvation," said the servant, "delights to meet you on this holy ground of Communion; and in these emblems, He gives you tokens of His love, and He pledges that this love shall never be withdrawn. Here, thirsty travelers are refreshed, troubled ones are comforted, the downcast are revived, and the weary and heavy-laden obtain rest."

As Pilgrim continued to partake of the feast that was spread before him, he exclaimed, "Lord, evermore give me this bread![5] I have more joy than the men of the world have, even when their corn, and their wine, and their oil, do most abound;[6] for 'I know whom I have believed, and am persuaded that he is able to keep that which I have committed unto him!'"[7]

"The Lord Immanuel," continued the servant, "desires to make this not only a place of *Commemoration,* but also a place of *Covenant!* While He seeks that these memorials should remind you of His dying love; He desires you also to renew here your engagements to be His only, and His wholly, and His forever!"

Then Pilgrim, arising from the table and lifting up his hands, swore by Him Who lives forever and ever, that no matter what others did – as for him, he would "serve the Lord!"[8]

"I have sworn," said he, "and will perform.[9] 'Who shall separate me from the love of Christ?'[10] I will follow You, O Great Captain of my salvation, whithersoever You see fit to lead me! 'Where thou goest I will go, and where thou dwellest I will dwell; thy people

---

[4] Genesis 28:16.
[5] John 6:34.
[6] Psalm 4:7.
[7] 2 Timothy 1:12.
[8] Joshua 24:15.
[9] Psalm 119:106.
[10] Romans 8:26.

shall be my people.'[11] Yea, death itself shall not separate between You and me!"

"The Lord Immanuel," replied the servant, "accepts the vows which your lips have uttered; and by these outward tokens, He ratifies – on His part – all of the blessings of the Covenant." So saying, I saw the ambassador of the King taking the charter which Pilgrim had received from Free Grace. He sealed it afresh with a golden signet; and the motto on it was this:

"BE THOU FAITHFUL UNTO DEATH, AND I WILL GIVE THEE
THE CROWN OF LIFE!"[12]

Precious to Pilgrim were these moments of communion upon the Mount of Ordinances! Often, he would interrupt the conversation, and exclaim, "Lord! It is good for me to be here!"[13] At last, Pilgrim and the servant began to descend the mountain path – the Lord's ambassador embracing him, and exhorting him to run with patience the race that was still set before him.[14] "Whenever your heart is overwhelmed, and in perplexity," said he, "look back to this Mount of Ordinances, and remember the glorious things which you saw and heard there."

"What!" exclaimed Pilgrim, in astonishment. "Do you speak of sorrow, and perplexity, and darkness, as yet awaiting me? I feel that this holy joy which I am now experiencing, can never be clouded! No man will ever be able to take it from me!"

"Alas!" replied the servant. "You know little of the pilgrimage in which you are engaged, if you suppose that your struggles and conflicts are at an end. Can you see," continued he, pointing to the golden towers of the New Jerusalem – "can you see yonder shining battlements? Never shall your spiritual joys be complete, and never shall your conflicts cease, until you are safe within those gates! This

---

[11] Ruth 1:16.
[12] Revelation 2:10.
[13] Matthew 17:4.
[14] Hebrews 12:1.

season which you have now enjoyed, is only a transient foretaste to refresh your spirit. It would not be well if it were otherwise. If no cloud were to disturb your present joys, it would lead you to forget your dependence upon an arm that is stronger than your own; and it would cause you to think that you had strength, when you actually have none. No, no; you must not yet speak of *rest* – that is not a word for earth. It is known only in heaven. Often, still, in this Valley of Tears, you will be covered with the scars of battle. Can you not, even now, discern that dense smoke?" continued he, pointing to a remote part of the landscape. "There lies the City of Carnality – the chief stronghold of the Prince of Darkness, wherein many unfortunate travelers have perished. The Narrow Way passes right through its streets; and its inhabitants – who are known by the name of 'Worldlings' – will lay wait for you, and try to sift you as wheat.[15] But fear not! The Lord of the Way will be with you! He has prayed for you, that your faith may not fail. His grace will be made sufficient for you.[16] Only be strong, and of a good courage. And the rest that remains for you within the gates of Zion, will be all the sweeter and more refreshing, by reason of the conflicts which have preceded it!"

So saying, the servant pronounced his benediction of peace; and Pilgrim, with tears of mingled joy and sorrow, parted from him to continue his journey. He felt that this season of communion was a foretaste of what was awaiting him within the gates of the Celestial City, when he would be "for ever with the Lord." Full of thankfulness, he went on his way praising and blessing God for all of the things which he had heard and seen – singing, as he went along, one of the loveliest of those songs which had been taught him by the Sweet Psalmist of Israel...

O send out thy light and thy truth: let them lead me;
Let them bring me unto thy holy hill, and to thy tabernacles.
Then will I go unto the altar of God – unto God, my exceeding joy:
Yea, upon the harp will I praise thee, O God, my God.

---

[15] Luke 22:31.
[16] 2 Corinthians 12:9.

The Great Journey

Why art thou cast down, O my soul? and why art thou
disquieted within me?
Hope in God: for I shall yet praise him, who is the health
of my countenance, and my God.[17]

---

[17] Psalm 43:3-5.

Questions for Thought - Chapter Seven

As Pilgrim thought of the ways in which God had hitherto helped him on his way, he set up a memorial-stone of remembrance. Can you think of a time in your life — perhaps after a time of affliction — when you have been able to reflect in awe upon the way in which God has sustained and kept you, and when you have experienced a sense of comfort that your Lord has not forsaken you? At such times, have you felt that the night of weeping has been worth enduring, in order to experience the joy of morning?

Upon the Mount of Ordinances, Pilgrim found a servant of Immanuel — standing ready to welcome him to partake of the emblems of the King's dying love "in remembrance" of Him, and to thereby nourish his soul. Pilgrims on the way to Zion need to be reminded often of the great salvation provided for them by Jesus. Have you ever noticed that actually sitting down and eating with someone is more of an intimate fellowship experience than merely meeting and exchanging greetings on the street? Do you find delight in availing yourself of Jesus' invitation to come and dine with Him, and to refresh your spirit by participating in Communion at His Table? Do we share Pilgrim's feelings when "he felt that this season of communion was a foretaste of what was awaiting him within the gates of the Celestial City, when he would be 'for ever with the Lord'"?

What did the King's servant warn Pilgrim about, after his meal on the Mount of Ordinances? Despite the joy and elation that we feel after being refreshed at the Lord's Table, we must still pass through this carnal world, which will try to ensnare us with its temptations. But what does the Lord of the Way do for us, to prevent our faith from failing? See Luke 22:31.

In the Cottage of Poverty | 8

Now I saw in my dream that, as evening drew on, Pilgrim was desirous of pausing at the nearest resting-place, in order to obtain lodging for the night. Wreaths of smoke ascending in the calm sky directed him to a village in the distance, which was concealed in the woods. The last beams of the sun were falling upon its humble abodes as he approached. Here and there, the lights in the little bay windows – blending with the lingering sunbeams – proclaimed the return of the peasant from his toil; while at times, the simple notes of an evening song of praise were wafted to Pilgrim's ear.

Approaching the first cottage of the hamlet by a wicket gate, he knocked and asked for admission.

"Who stands outside?" inquired a gentle voice from within.

"A traveler to Mount Zion," replied Pilgrim, "who is fleeing from the wrath to come, and claims that hospitality which was never denied by one humble follower of the Lord Immanuel to another."

"Neither shall it be so now," answered the speaker, unbarring the door and disclosing the figure of an aged woman, who was simply attired. Her name was Poverty; and a little handmaid, named Contentment, shared with her the frugal comforts of her lot. Upon the entrance, above the doorway, Pilgrim observed these words inscribed:

"A LITTLE THAT A JUST MAN HATH IS BETTER
THAN THE RICHES OF MANY WICKED."

Now I saw that after the inhabitants of the cottage had assisted Pilgrim in washing his feet, and had provided him with necessary refreshment; they entered into mutual conversation about their respective histories and conditions.

"You seem," said Pilgrim (addressing the elder of the two), "to be strangers to many outward comforts; and yet I believe that you are happier disciples of the Lord Immanuel than any others whom I have seen during the entire course of my journey!"

"We *are* indeed poor in this world," replied Poverty. "But God has made us to be rich in *faith,* and heirs together of the kingdom of heaven.[1] I feel that in this village of Godliness, with my handmaid Contentment, I have 'great gain.'"

"But," said Pilgrim, "I think I remember one who shared the same name with you – perhaps he was a relative of yours. He was a Broad-Way-traveler, who seemed of all men the most miserable. He was accompanied by two associates, called Improvidence and Vice; and he was an object of abhorrence – even to the worst of the Broad-Way-men!

"Alas!" replied Poverty. "If I was bereaved of God, I would be bereaved indeed; there is no condition that is more pitiable than *godless poverty,* and there is none that is more blessed than *poverty when sanctified.* 'The Lord is my portion,' and I feel that I need no other."

"What an enviable lot!" exclaimed Pilgrim. "You also seem to be blessed with devout neighbors; but if they are as poor as yourself, I see not how they can find time for the service of the Lord Immanuel, in the midst of their daily toil."

"Where there is a will, there is a way," answered the other. "You will generally find that the man who is most diligent in business, is also the most fervent in serving the Lord. Besides, in our lowly estate, there are fewer prizes which worldly ambition holds out to us; and therefore, we have greater inducement to seek our treasure in heaven. We have fewer of the 'many things' about which to be 'careful and troubled,' and we have more leisure to think of the 'one thing needful.'"

"I am certain, also, that in yonder precious volume," continued Pilgrim, pointing to the sole occupant of the table – "I am certain

---

[1] James 2:5.

that in that great Guide-Book to Immanuel's land, you will find much to make you rejoice that this lowly condition has been yours."

"Yes, indeed!" replied she. "Our lot is a blessed one; because in its very lowliness, we are like our Divine Master! The Lord Immanuel Himself was a poor man. For our sakes, He became poor[2] — so poor, that while the foxes had holes, and the birds of the air had nests, the Son of Man had no place to lay His head."[3]

"Most true," said Pilgrim. "Besides, I have always thought it one of the wonders of that sacred Volume," he continued — pointing towards the Book at their side — "that it is emphatically the poor man's."

"Yes, truly," replied Poverty. "While it contains the noblest and sublimest truths; it also contains truths so plain and simple, that the humblest can understand them. When reading of Prophets and Apostles, and of the Lord of Apostles — I feel that I am following the footsteps of the poor. Thus I see that poverty can have no disgrace, for it was honored and sanctified by the Lord Immanuel Himself — who chose it as His only birthright."

Thus Pilgrim continued his conversation with his humble hosts, until the fatigues of the day induced him to retire to rest. As morning dawned, he once more resumed his journey — leaving behind a memorial of gratitude for the kindness bestowed upon him; and receiving, in recompense, the parting benediction of grateful hearts: "Blessed is he that considereth the poor!"[4]

---

[2] 2 Corinthians 8:9.
[3] Matthew 8:20.
[4] Psalm 41:1.

Questions for Thought – Chapter Eight

What was the difference between the woman named Poverty in the lowly cottage, and the traveler in the Broad-Way who went by that same name?

Poverty and Contentment describe their situation as a blessed and enviable one. Why? Does it change your outlook on the contrast between wealth and poverty when you realize that poverty in itself is not a sin; and that those who are in such a condition are very much like our Lord Jesus, Who was so poor that He had nowhere to lay His head?

Do you find wealth and "much stuff" to be a burdensome thing? Do you find poverty and a "lack of stuff" to be hard to endure? The key to happiness — no matter how much or how little of this world's physical possessions we enjoy — is to be found in the grace of contentment. What does Paul tell Timothy about contentment, in 1 Timothy 6:6? Do you think that it is easier to be content when we remember promises such as those which our Savior gives us in Matthew 6:31-33?

Visiting the King's Hospital | 9

Now I saw in my dream that Pilgrim pursued his journey without interruption until nightfall. His path led through a succession of wooded glades, which were intersected occasionally with marshy ground. As he proceeded, the country began to have few traces of human habitations – until even a shepherd and his flock were rarely seen to relieve the solitude. And the only refreshment that Pilgrim himself could obtain, was at the streams of water which crossed the way now and then. As the shadows of evening began to fall, he arrived at a secluded place in the center of a forest – where a large building stood, called The King's Hospital. In this place, travelers who had grown weak or faint, or who had been wounded by enemies, resorted for cure to "the Great Physician" – by which name, the Lord Immanuel was here known. Nor was the Hospital restricted to Narrow-Way-men only. Occasionally, some Broad-Way-travelers who had been wounded by the arrows of conviction, or who were fainting under trial, sought shelter in this place. But in their case, the residence was brief; for – not submitting to the Physician's cure, and preferring false ones of their own – they soon returned to the way of destruction.

Now I saw that one of the servants of the Great Physician conducted Pilgrim to a large hall in the Hospital, which was filled with beds and couches. Upon these, the sick and wounded were laid. Some of them were groaning heavily; others were lying with pale lips and sunken eyes, scarcely able to endure the feeble light that was admitted from above; and still others cast an imploring look of mercy towards the door, as they saw the newcomer enter.

"We shall first visit the ward where the more hopeless patients are laid," explained Pilgrim's conductor. "They are Broad-Way-men, who have been driven by fear – or often, by the stunning blow of trial – to take temporary refuge here. But they endure for only a little while.[1] Their hearts get hardened, and their latter end is worse with them than the beginning! But follow me," continued he. "Perhaps the admonition of a Narrow-Way-traveler, like yourself, may induce them to think of their awful peril and danger."

The first bedside at which they stood was that of a patient called Self-Righteousness. "This," said Pilgrim's guide, "is a man who now imagines himself to be 'rich, and having need of nothing.' But you yourself can see that he is 'wretched, and miserable, and naked.'"[2]

Upon approaching the patients' couch, Pilgrim's attendant offered the sick man some white linen, which had been prescribed by the Great Physician to staunch the blood flowing from a wound in his side. But the sufferer tore it away; and he persisted, instead, in binding it with some filthy rags which were scattered on his pillow.

In the same ward, there was also another patient by the same name. He was not laid upon a bed like the other; instead, with a haughty air, he was pacing the floor of the hall in which he was confined. A hectic flush covered his face – such as the one that deceives the consumption patient, when he mistakes the token of death as a sign of returning health. His miserable clothing was relieved here and there by a bright patch of gaudy tinsel, which only made the rest appear more wretched. "There," said the conductor, "is a poor deluded maniac. He imagines himself to be the heir of a kingdom, while he is the most miserable of beggars."

Now I saw that Faithful (for that was the name of the attendant) approached Self-Righteousness; and he invited him to come to the opposite side of the chamber, where there was a large mirror called the "Mirror of the Law." Into this looking-glass, Faithful urged him to look – but in vain. "This mirror," he explained, addressing Pilgrim, "is the grand means of disclosing to such patients their real

---

[1] Mark 4:17.
[2] Revelation 3:17.

condition. As long as they continue 'measuring themselves by themselves, and comparing themselves among themselves,'[3] there is little hope of recovery. But by this Law-Mirror, they obtain a knowledge of sin;[4] and they become convinced that unless they have another clothing of righteousness than their own, 'they will in no case enter into the kingdom of heaven!'[5] Among others, there once was a person of great fame in the Narrow Way, who gloried in his rags of self-righteousness for a long time. But no sooner did he stand before that Law-Mirror, than he burst into tears and exclaimed, 'I was alive once, before I came to that mirror! But when its reflection showed me my vileness, sin came alive; and I found myself to be spiritually dead!'"[6]

Passing on from these patients, Pilgrim and his conductor moved to another bed, where a patient by the name of Indifference lay. His countenance had an even more ghastly appearance than those whom they had already witnessed. His pale cheeks and drooping eyes revealed that death was indeed close at hand.

"You are madly trifling with your eternal all!" cried Faithful, unwilling to pass by the bed of the deluded man without a word of admonition. "You are hovering on the border of two worlds! Do you not consider that the breath of your nostrils is all that is between you and the bar of God?" But, being reckless of his situation, Indifference smiled at the fears of his attendants. With cold and heartless concern, he received the warnings that were sent to him by the Great Physician; and then, turning himself over on his pillow, he pursued his idle song.

At his side lay a miserable man named Despair – a painful contrast to the other. Unlike Indifference, he was not insensible to his condition! On the contrary, his groans and cries rung piteously throughout the hall! Once and again, Pilgrim's attendant attempted

---

[3] 2 Corinthians 10:12.
[4] Romans 3:26.
[5] Matthew 5:20.
[6] Romans 7:9.

to mix a soothing drink, and present it to his lips. It would have given him immediate relief; but he dashed it to the ground – wringing his hands, and exclaiming, "Undone! Undone!" Faithful, the attendant, tried to remonstrate. He assured the patient that there was still hope; for in representing his case to the Great Physician, he had received this reply: "I have no pleasure in his death, but far rather that he would turn and live!"[7]

"No," replied the agonized sufferer; "the medicine which might heal others can be of no avail for me! Let the footsteps of Death approach when they may – my doom is sealed! To dream of recovery is vain."

"Neither your name nor your language, unhappy man," said Pilgrim, "should be heard here. *Despair* is not a word for earth! It is known only in the bottomless pit. Giant Despair is the gloomy warden of that place where hope never enters; and it is only when he turns his key, and leaves you in the blackness of eternal darkness, that you can disbelieve the efficacy of the Great Physician. He is now able to save 'even to the uttermost!'[8] Where is the patient that He has either failed or refused to cure?"

But the poor man would not listen to expostulation. He wrapped himself in his bedclothes; wrung his hands again; and cried louder than ever, "Lost! Lost! Lost!"

Now I saw that Pilgrim and his escort next stood at the bedside of a patient called Procrastination – a relative of the traveler whom Pilgrim had met outside the Narrow-Way-Gate. He was laid on his back, breathing heavily; and the symptoms of death were quickly gathering around his pillow. "This," explained Faithful, "is an example of the folly of delaying to adopt the prescribed remedy. Here is a man who received a wound in his hand, which he considered too trifling to demand attention. He urged one night's delay, but delay has only aggravated the suffering. The fatal symptoms increase, and now the venom has spread through his whole arm. Poor patient!"

---

[7] Ezekiel 18:32.
[8] Hebrews 7:25.

continued Faithful, addressing the sufferer. "Will it not be far better for you – if your right hand offends you – to cut it off and cast it from you, and to enter into life maimed; than to have your whole body thrown into hell-fire?"[9]

"Yet one more night," feebly whispered the patient. "And to-morrow, I promise to submit."

"Tomorrow," said Faithful, "may come; but it will come too late! *Today,* if you will hear the voice of the Great Physician, harden not your heart.[10] Behold! *Now* is the accepted time;[11] for you may rest assured that by the time another night has passed, your pulse will be still, and you will be beyond the reach of both physician and cure."

"Well, perhaps," replied the other (who was unwilling to offend, and yet reluctant to submit) – "perhaps before evening comes, I may consent. But 'go thy way' for this time, at least; 'at a more convenient season, I will call for thee.'"[12] And so saying, Procrastination once more closed his eyes, and left Pilgrim and his guide to continue on.

Besides these patients, there were other sufferers of a different but more hopeful kind. In a secluded part of the hall, which was dimly lighted by a grated window, Pilgrim beheld a patient who *had* been renewed in the spirit of his mind; but nevertheless, he seemed to be as much in distress as many of the others. Pilgrim observed that a lifeless corpse was fastened, by an iron chain, to this man's body. He had been obliged to drag this burden behind him for a great part of the Narrow Way. But the weight was so great, that he had been compelled to take refuge in the Hospital for a few days, in order to strengthen his weak frame. The dead body was in a putrid state, and it was loathsome to look upon; and always and again, it

---

[9] Matthew 18:8.

[10] Psalm 95:8.

[11] 2 Corinthians 6:2.

[12] Acts 24:25.

extracted from the sufferer this plaintive cry: "O wretched man that I am! Who shall deliver me from this body of death?"[13]

"How is it," inquired Pilgrim, addressing this man, "that you have come to be subjected to such a burden?"

"This," replied the man, "is called Original Sin. Its weight, as you may well believe, forms a fearful drag to me as I pursue my journey – so much so, that I am sometimes tempted to resign the struggle. And yet they tell me that although it is gradually wasting away, I cannot expect it to be finally removed until I am safe within the Celestial City."

"But," inquired Pilgrim, "cannot the Lord of the Way give you liberty at once, by breaking these chains which bind you to this lifeless body?"

"Yes," replied the other. "His power and His compassion are equally boundless; but He tells me that the remains of Original Sin will continue to cling to my earthly nature, until the day which brings me safely within the gates of Mount Zion."

"What were the reasons that He assigned for this?" asked Pilgrim.

"They were various," answered the man. "Some of them were to keep me mindful that this Valley of Tears is not my home; and to make me long for that land where the chains of corruption, which fetter the spirit here, can shackle and impair its energies no more. Another reason was to preserve a continual sense of my own weakness, and of my total dependence upon the Great Physician. But," continued he – a gleam of joy brightening his countenance – "the heavier the irons in the prison-house of earth, the sweeter the liberty of heaven! In this tabernacle, I groan and am burdened;[14] but it is my consolation to think that this body of sin and death will be unknown, as soon as I am finally safe within yonder walls. O for the

---

[13] Romans 7:24.
[14] 2 Corinthians 5:4.

arrival of that blessed hour, when this corruptible shall put on incorruption; and this mortal, immortality; and mortality shall be swallowed up in life!"

Now I saw in my dream that Pilgrim was conducted by Faithful into another chamber. "This," said his guide, "is a room appropriated for the use of aged and infirmed travelers, who – on account of their years – are unable to continue their journey any farther."

Upon entering the room, Pilgrim beheld an individual whose hair was whitened with age. The armor with which the veteran warrior was still girded, showed the marks of many hard encounters; but it had lost none of its brightness. His sword exhibited a blunted edge, and yet it gleamed with a brilliancy that was just as dazzling as it was on the day when it was unsheathed in the armory at the Narrow-Way-Gate. Pilgrim approached the man, just as the last tear that he had to shed was standing in his eye. "It is enough!" said he. "Now, Lord, lettest thou thy servant depart in peace."[15] A serene smile suffused the man's countenance; his eye was fixed upon the

---

[15] Luke 2:29.

gates of the Celestial City. While other objects around him were growing dim, this glorious vision seemed to be brightening. "Go on!" said the man, addressing Pilgrim. "Go on in this Narrow Way that leadeth unto life; and take the assurance of one who has trodden it for a long time, that it is indeed a way of pleasantness, and a path of peace.[16] 'I have fought a good fight,'" continued the departing saint – raising himself once more, with the last glow of life beaming upon his face. "'I have fought a good fight; I have finished my course; I have kept the faith: henceforth there is laid up for me a crown of righteousness, which the Lord, the Righteous Judge, will give me on that day.'[17] We shall meet no more until we meet within the gates of yonder Celestial City. Farewell! Farewell!" He uttered one parting groan; and the next moment, he was sleeping sweetly in Jesus.

Now I saw that angels were waiting with a chariot – ready to carry the soul of the saint to the gates of Mount Zion. Pilgrim's eyes followed the bright retinue, until the last of the procession was lost in the glories which encompassed the New Jerusalem.

Returning again to the chamber which they had just left, Pilgrim and his conductor approached a patient whose name was Sorrow. She was arrayed in a black cloak, and she had a tear upon her cheek. At her side sat Resignation – the same benevolent and pious woman whom Pilgrim had met while passing through the Fiery Furnace. Resignation had a Book in her hand – from the pages of which, she was endeavoring to soothe her companion, who sat brooding in silent dejection over the wreck of some treasured joys.

"Not long ago," said Faithful, "this woman dwelt in an arbor near the City of Carnality. At one time, it was trellised and adorned with some of the loveliest plants which the Valley could supply. Shady gourds combined with flowers of various tints and fragrance, in order to spread a covering over her head, and to form a shade

---

[16] Proverbs 3:17.
[17] 2 Timothy 4:7.

from the noonday sun. But in an unexpected moment, a canker-worm feasted upon the roots. One bud alone survived, when the rest had perished. But this, too, has just been plucked by the hand of Death; and now, as you see, it lies ruined and withered at her feet. But since her earthly flowers have perished, this woman has come here seeking the Rose of Sharon and the Lily of the Valley.[18] She has come to have her heart soothed with the Balm of Gilead,[19] which she has heard that the Great Physician applies to bleeding hearts."

Now I saw that when Pilgrim stepped closer, he heard Resignation singing – in plaintive tones – the following lines to her companion:

"Why weep for the beautiful flower,
As if premature plucked away?
Survived had its blossoms that hour,
'Twould have lived, but have lived to decay!

But now it has left this cold scene
To blossom in regions above;
Where no storm, where no clouds intervene
To darken the sunshine of love!

Oh! Happy, thrice happy, the time
When again ye shall meet, ne'er to sever,
With that flower, in that happier clime,
To bask in bright sunshine forever!"

"Yes," said Resignation, dwelling upon the last words that she had uttered; "wait until that day of cloudless sunshine, and 'in God's light thou wilt see light.' Then you will be brought to confess that He was 'righteous in all his ways, and holy in all his works.'"[20]

---

[18] Song of Solomon 2:1.
[19] Jeremiah 8:22.
[20] Psalm 114:17.

"'His way,' indeed, seems to be 'in the sea,'" replied the other; "'and his path in the deep waters, and his judgments unsearchable.' But I know that the Lord of the Way doeth 'all things well.'"

"Yes," said Resignation. "He Himself will be a richer portion than any earthly one. The Living Fountain will supply the broken cistern!"

"I have found it! I have found it!" exclaimed the weeping mourner, rejoicing through her tears. "The Great Physician has cheered my solitary hours with His own blessed presence, and lighted up this heart with untold joy. I never knew the tenderness of His dealings until now. He seems to be 'touched with a feeling of all my infirmities.'"[21]

"And I think that you can bear testimony," observed Pilgrim, "that you obtained no cordial to heal your aching heart, until you received it from Him."

"None! None!" replied Sorrow. "Every other earthly joy seemed to be only a mockery. Earthly refuges were refuges of lies. Earthly comforters sought in vain to soothe my woes. But when I came seeking the Balm in Gilead, and the Physician there; He said these words to me: 'I will not leave you comfortless. Peace I leave with you, my peace I give unto you: not as the world giveth.'"[22]

"What else said He unto you?" inquired Pilgrim.

"He told me," replied Sorrow, "what His own precious name once was: 'the man of sorrows.'[23] He said that there was not a pang that I could feel, that His own holy heart had not felt as well; and He told me that in all my afflictions, He had been afflicted likewise.[24] And when I spoke to Him of my crosses and losses, He answered me in tones of tender rebuke: 'Was there any sorrow like unto my sorrow?'"[25]

---

[21] Hebrews 4:15.

[22] John 14:18, 27.

[23] Isaiah 53:3.

[24] Isaiah 63:9.

[25] Lamentations 1:12.

"I see that you feel," said Pilgrim, "as all of His suffering people have felt – that the Lord of the Way makes up for the loss of earthly blessings."

"I do," answered the other. "'The Lord is my Shepherd, I shall not want!'[26] Many have been my trials; and every day, this Valley of Tears seems truer to its own name. But – God be thanked – amidst the wreck of earthly blessings, I still have the better Friend – Jesus Christ, Who is the same yesterday, and today, and forever."[27]

"'Whom the Lord loveth,'" said Resignation, still reading from the Volume which she held in her hands, "'he chasteneth, and scourgeth every son whom he receiveth.'[28] 'He afflicteth not willingly, nor grieveth the children of men.'[29] 'We know that all things work together for good to them that love God, to them who are the called according to his purpose.'[30] 'What I do thou knowest not now, but thou shalt know hereafter.'"[31]

"'Even so!'" replied the submissive sufferer, clasping her hands. "'Even so, Father; for so it seemeth good in thy sight.'[32] 'I will be dumb; I will open not my mouth, because thou didst it.'[33] 'Not as I will, but as thou wilt.'[34] 'The Lord gave, and the Lord taketh away; blessed be the name of the Lord!'"[35]

Before Pilgrim departed, he was refreshed and strengthened by the Lord of the Way; and he was again warned of the dangers which he would have to encounter in the city which had been pointed out to him from the Mount of Communion. Then he started out, with renewed ardor, upon the portion of the journey which yet remained

---

[26] Psalm 23:1.
[27] Hebrews 13:8.
[28] Hebrews 12:6.
[29] Lamentations 3:33.
[30] Romans 8:28.
[31] John 13:7.
[32] Matthew 11:26.
[33] Psalm 39:9.
[34] Luke 22:39.
[35] Job 1:21.

— cheered with the prospect of the glorious crown, which the Lord of the Way held out as the covenanted reward of the "faithful unto death."[36]

---

[36] Revelation 2:10.

John Ross MacDuff

Questions for Thought - Chapter Nine

What did Faithful try to get the second patient by the name of Self-Righteousness to look at? What does this object do, and why is it such a good and necessary (although uncomfortable) thing for us to see it? Who was the "person of great fame in the Narrow Way" that Faithful was describing, "who gloried in his rags of self-righteousness for a long time," until he stood before that Mirror? See Romans 7:9.

What was the name of the patient who was dressed in a black cloak, with tears on her cheeks? Who was the companion was that was sitting at her side, and from what Book do you think she was reading? Whose beloved presence became Sorrow's remedy — causing her to exclaim, "I have found it! I have found it!"

When we encounter ill and hurting people in our lifetime, do we do the best that we possibly can to minister to their needs — regardless of our opinions concerning them? Hopefully, we are not like the priest and the Levite in our Lord's Good Samaritan parable, who walked "on the other side" in order to avoid helping the wounded man. Are we ready to comfort and direct those who are hurting to the Great Physician, like Resignation did with Sorrow?

Meeting
Theophilus　|　10

Now I saw in my dream that before Pilgrim had advanced far, he was overtaken by a fellow-traveler. He was girded from head to foot with the Christian armor, and his eye was steadily directed to the gate of the Celestial City. So eagerly, indeed, did he pursue his way, that he would have passed Pilgrim without noticing him – except that his attention was attracted by one of the Songs of Zion, with which Pilgrim was cheering himself on this solitary part of the road.

"Where are you headed, my good traveler?" inquired the other man, addressing Pilgrim. "It seems from your attire, as well as your song, that you are a brother journeying to Immanuel's land."

"You have guessed rightly," said Pilgrim. "And I was even now comforting myself with the thought that so much of the wilderness is behind me, and that the time is so near at hand when these weapons of warfare will be needed no longer. I am enfeebled by many wounds, but one hour within yonder gates will make me forget them all. Therefore, 'though faint, I am still pursuing';[1] and I have the assurance of my heavenly Lord and Master, that final victory will at length be mine!"

"You speak well," replied the other, "and as if love to the Lord of the Way truly burned in your heart! So crowded is this Narrow Way nowadays with false professors – ever since a powerful potentate, called Fashion, tore down the wall of separation which formerly divided it from the Broad Way – that I cannot help regarding its alleged travelers with suspicion, in case they should be Broad-Way-men in disguise. But," continued he, "I am persuaded better things of you, and things which accompany salvation, although I thus

---

[1] Judges 8:4.

speak.[2] Perhaps if we pursue our journey together, we may prove – by the blessing of our common King – to be comforters in each other's sorrows, and helpers of each other's joys."

"Gladly," replied Pilgrim, "will I accept your offered friendship; for truly, my spirit trembles with fear as I behold the smoke of yonder City of Carnality darkening the plain, and as I think of the evils that may likely befall me there."

"Never fear!" replied the other man. "You have a stronger arm than that of a fellow-traveler to lean upon, and to conduct you safely through its dangers. But in the meantime, as we pursue our journey, let us recount our experiences of the Lord's kindness, in order that we may be so much the better prepared for the trials which may await us in that city. I pray you," continued he, "tell me your history! Tell me when it was that the Lord of the Way mercifully first snatched you from destruction, and arrayed you in your present attire."

Here Pilgrim minutely related the marvelous interposition of the Lord Immanuel, as well as the other manifestations of grace which he had subsequently experienced. The other traveler, at intervals, could not repress his feelings. And Pilgrim himself felt that his own gratitude was heightened and increased, as he called afresh to his recollection the wondrous things that the King of the Way had done for him.

"Be pleased, kind friend," said Pilgrim, after he had concluded his own narration, "to recount to me, in turn, the adventures which have befallen you in your journey. What is your name? And what first induced you to turn your face Zion-ward?"

"My name," answered the other, "was once Neglecter; but it has been changed by the King of the Way into Theophilus, which means 'Lover of God.' The place of my birth was close to your own, in a village very near to the Broad Road. I was the familiar friend and companion of those very men whom you met with on your way – Formality, Church-goer, and Almost-persuaded; and I was induced,

---

[2] Hebrews 6:9.

like yourself, to adopt their creed. I thought my own religion, on average, far above my neighbors'; for I was not a *despiser,* as most of them were, but only a *Forgetter.*[3] I was not an *enemy* to salvation, but I only *neglected* it; and hence my name."

"But," asked Pilgrim, "were there none in your own household to remind you of your danger, and of the consequences of such neglect?"

"Alas!" cried Theophilus. "In my case, it was only too true that a man's foes are those of his own household. My own awakened convictions would have often roused me from my sloth, had they not been overborne by those who professed to love me the most. They told me that I was as good as others; that I had reasons which other men did not have (namely, urgency of business) for postponing the question of my salvation; and that if I would only have patience, the time was coming when they would all join me, and seek it in good earnest."

"And how, then," inquired Pilgrim, "were you at last roused to a sense of your awful danger?"

"Ah!" replied the other. "The merciful Lord Immanuel would not allow me to get rest by day, nor sleep by night, by reason of His loud and earnest remonstrances. The mingled severity and sweetness of His entreaties is still sounding in my ears!"

"How did He speak with you?" asked Pilgrim.

"So great was His love," answered Theophilus, "and so resolved was He to effect my rescue, that He sent messenger after messenger to my door,[4] to plead for admission. He knocked by Providence, by Affliction, by Bereavement, by Prosperity, and by Adversity; and each one of these – in a voice louder than the ones before – sounded the question in my ears: 'How shall ye escape if ye neglect such great salvation?'[5] That question gave me no peace. It followed me in my solitary walks, it crowded my waking hours by day, and it disturbed

---

[3] Hebrews 2:3.
[4] Revelation 3:20.
[5] Hebrews 2:3.

my dreams by night! I tried to drown it in the cup of intemperance, and to chase it away amidst scenes of mirth; but if I succeeded in hushing it at night, it was sure to return upon me – louder than ever – in the morning!"

"And what said your family all this while?" asked Pilgrim. "Did they not observe your anxiety of mind, and make some effort to minister comfort to you?"

"Miserable comforters they were,"[6] replied Theophilus. "They called me a madman and a fool, they laughed at my childish anxieties, and they only invited new guests to banish what they called my 'fit of frenzy' away."

"But I have just interrupted you. I long to hear the result!"

"Well," continued Theophilus, "as I lay one night stretched upon my bed, the messenger called Affliction was once more sent by the Lord Immanuel to renew her accustomed knockings. Never before were they so long nor so loud – so loud, indeed, that even some of my own family were startled from their slumbers. Now it so happened that I had two servants in the house; the name of one was Conscience, and the name of the other was Will. Both of them were aroused by the knockings, and they ran to the door to inquire concerning the errand of the person standing outside. Conscience no sooner listened to her words of tenderness and kind expostulation, than she was desirous to grant her admittance. But Will, who was naturally of a depraved and obstinate disposition, stoutly remonstrated; and – being the stronger of the two – she put her back to the door, secured the lock, and refused to open it."

"How well I understand the struggle you describe!" said Pilgrim. "But say on."

"You are acquainted, I presume," continued the other, "with one of the Lord Immanuel's servants in the Narrow Way Hospital, named Faithful."

"I am," was the reply; "and I think that you would find him as faithful by nature as he is by name."

---

[6] Job 16:2.

"Faithful, indeed," proceeded Theophilus; "for no sooner was he acquainted with my case, and with the strange conflict in my heart, than he came to assist Affliction in her knockings. With a large hammer – called the Hammer of the Word – which he wielded in his hands, he broke open the door! He stood by my bedside with his hands and lips full of messages of mercy from the Master he served, and he never left me until he had brought me to the Narrow-Way-Gate."

"But," asked Pilgrim, "were you allowed to leave without an effort being made for your rescue?"

"Of course not!" replied Theophilus. "My companions, neighbors, and friends came running after me with imploring voices – some entreating me to return; some using threatenings; others ridicule; others bribes. My wife and children, with tears in their eyes, employed every persuasive measure to induce me to return. But the Lord of the Way sent His messenger to whisper these words in my ear: 'Whosoever leaveth father, and mother, and wife, and children, and houses, and lands, for my name's sake, and the Gospel, shall receive in this life an hundredfold, and in the world to come, life everlasting.'[7] 'But whosoever loveth father and mother, or wife and children, more than me, is not worthy of me!'"[8]

"And did you have to wait long at the entrance-gate?" inquired Pilgrim.

"No; for Free Grace, the Keeper, was in readiness for my reception. At that time, only one other traveler was asking for admission; for the crowd was all flocking down the opposite way to Destruction. The traveler's name was Waverer; he was a native of the border-country that lies between King Immanuel's territories and those of the Prince of Darkness. He had a bundle upon his back, containing heart-lusts, heart-sins, and heart-idols; he valued these too much to be induced to part with them, and yet he seemed

---

[7] Mark 10:29, 30.
[8] Matthew 11:37.

equally reluctant to abandon the Way of Life. He would have willingly entered, provided that he could have retained his bundle. But it was too large; the gate was too narrow to admit it. So he turned down the Broad Road, and I saw his face no more."

"Wretched man!" exclaimed Pilgrim. "I remember him well, and I truly think that he is to be pitied more than any of his fellow-Broad-Way-men; for he knows just enough of the Narrow Way to make him miserable, but not enough to give him peace. From his sad fate, let us learn the danger of trifling with besetting sins."

"And doubtless," continued Pilgrim, "you can add your experience to mine, concerning the Lord of the Way. Since the first hour that you were enrolled in His service – no matter how faithless you may have been to *Him* – He has never been unfaithful to *you*."

"It is true; it is very true!" answered Theophilus, with the tears again starting to his eyes. "So often have I wounded His loving heart, and so often have I fainted and been weary of Him; but never has He fainted or been weary of me! When I am called to mourn the fickleness of my own heart, it is my consolation that His heart never changes!"[9]

Now I saw in my dream that as the two fellow-travelers thus continued to encourage one another with mutual experiences of the Lord's past kindnesses to them, they gradually approached the walls of the great metropolis of the City of Carnality – the smoke of which had been pointed out to Pilgrim from the Mount of Ordinances. It seemed to cast a temporary gloom over their spirits, as they thought how speedily their conversation was to be interrupted by the din and bustle of this city of abounding iniquity. But with their eyes uplifted to the Everlasting Hills, whose summits were crowned with the glittering battlements of Zion; and with a firm confidence in the Lord of the Way – the two travelers boldly approached its walls.

---

[9] Malachi 3:6.

Questions for Thought – Chapter Ten

What an encouragement Pilgrim found when he met a fellow-traveler on the road to Immanuel's land! What was the new name that this fellow-pilgrim had been given? Have you ever met a fellow-believer who was not from your local church, and perhaps not even from the same denomination; but nevertheless, you instantly knew, "This person is a genuine son or daughter of the King!" If you have had this kind of experience, what have you centered your fellowship in? Has it been Jesus? Has it been a struggle for you to not key in on your "differences" instead?

Why did Theophilus regard Pilgrim with suspicion at first? What do you think he meant when he said that Fashion had torn down the wall separating the Narrow Way from the Broad Way? Do you think that this might be the case today – especially in Western society – where it is so "fashionable" to "be a Christian" that nearly everyone professes to be one, even if they are living in an openly sinful lifestyle?

Everyone has their own testimony of how the Lord saved them from their sins and called them to salvation. Some can only tell you that they were brought up from an early age to love the Lord Jesus, and to trust in Him for redemption from their sins; while with others, their conversion was much more of a dramatic and sensational experience. How and when did you come to trust the good news of the Savior's Gospel? It's important to remember, though, that the great focus of our "testimony" should not be a focus on ourselves; but rather, upon the amazing grace and love of Christ! And if He expended so much effort to draw us to Himself, even when our sinful nature resisted Him (like Theophilus); how greatly do you think He will "hold on to us" eternally?

The City of Carnality | 11

Now I saw in my dream that the Narrow Way went straight through the City of Carnality; for the Prince of Darkness (who, from the extent of his territories, was called "the god of this world"[1]) had built many cities and villages close by the wayside, for the purpose of enticing Zion-ward travelers, if possible. And at the time of Pilgrim's journey, he could accomplish this goal more easily; for the walls which had separated the Broad-Way-men from the Narrow-Way-travelers in former times, had been mostly demolished. For a long time, a deadly enmity had existed between them. But the vice-regent of the Prince of Darkness, whose name was Fashion, had interposed as mediator between the contending parties. It was now counted no disgrace (as it had been formerly) for a Broad-Way-man to be visibly enlisted in Immanuel's ranks. But the Narrow-Way-men suffered by their guilty compromise; for their interaction with the Broad-Way-travelers had caused them to imbibe many carnal maxims and principles, and to conform to the practices of a "world lying in wickedness."[2]

Now I saw that the Prince of Darkness had erected his metropolis near the end of the Valley of Tears. And although travelers who had received the Charter at the Narrow-Way-Gate could not fall a sacrifice to his tricks (being preserved by the special grace of the Lord of the Way), yet many who had given fair promise of seeking Zion – and that, too, with their faces thitherward – were entangled by the snares laid for them in this city; and they never advanced a step nearer to the Celestial gates.

---

[1] 2 Corinthians 4:4.
[2] 1 John 5:19.

The shadows of evening were beginning to fall as Pilgrim and his companion approached the walls of the City of Carnality. Even from the twilight-glimpse that they obtained, they were awed by its dimensions and magnificence. In the center, crowning the heights, they beheld a palace with a royal banner waving from its towers; and many lights were gleaming from the windows of its banqueting halls. This (as Pilgrim afterwards learned) was the residence of Free-thinker – a powerful vassal of the King of the Broad Way. He had been rewarded with ample honors for the service which he had rendered to his lord. The porter of this palace was called Mammon; and he made it his business to exact as large a revenue as he possibly could for the Prince of Darkness, whose servant he was. The two travelers trembled as they stood in the presence of this man, who was of a harsh and repulsive countenance. Upon attempting to pass, he rudely approached them; and with a rough voice, he demanded payment of tribute for the King's Highway.

"We are travelers to Mount Zion," answered Theophilus; "and the Lord Immanuel, in order to secure our admittance there, hath already paid costlier tribute-money than we have to offer. We have not been redeemed 'with corruptible things such as silver and gold,' and the Celestial City is not to be purchased with such materials."[3]

"If you have no tribute-money," replied the porter, "it will be necessary to at least leave behind you, as a pledge, some part of your armor. During your sojourn in the city, it will only encumber you; and it will be restored to you upon your return."

"Return we cannot – we dare not!" exclaimed Pilgrim. "We have our faces set Zion-wards, and woe be to us if we turn back!"[4]

Now I saw that an unseen hand from behind touched Pilgrim's shoulder and urged him to follow without delay. He was reluctant to leave his companion without making an effort to secure his safety also, for he still unwisely continued his disputation at the gate. But the person behind him was persistent in her demands to tarry not a

---

[3] 1 Peter 1:18.
[4] Luke 9:62.

moment longer; and Pilgrim, dreading further delay, followed her footsteps.

After retracing part of the way, Pilgrim was taken along a narrow path to a lodging-house by the side of the city wall. He was conducted within by his guide, whose name was Piety; she resided there with her sister, named Devotion. They assisted their visitor in brightening his armor, wiped the dust from his sandals, and replenished his traveler's bag with some simple victuals. After this, they warned him of the imminent dangers with which he would be beset; and they exhorted Pilgrim to "consider him" Who Himself had once been a pilgrim in that same city, and Who "had endured such contradiction of sinners against himself."[5] And they directed him up the streets to the residence of the Christian Graces, at the gate on the opposite side of the city; where he would again be refreshed, and receive further directions regarding his journey.

Now I saw that Pilgrim proceeded boldly into the heart of the town, and he had penetrated a considerable way before he encountered any serious trouble.

Before long, however, the citizens began to be attracted by the peculiarity of his traveling attire. A crowd followed — some mocking; some deriding; some even lifting the mud and filth from off the streets, and besmearing his armor. He tried first to remonstrate with them, and then to rebuke and threaten. With the Sword of the Spirit[6] grasped firmly in his hand, he succeeded in deflecting many of the blows aimed at him; and their stones and missiles rebounded from the Shield of Faith,[7] with which he covered his head. And he felt it no small encouragement when his eye fell on one of the verses inscribed underneath the shield: "If ye were of the world, the world would love its own; but because ye are not of the world, but I have chosen you out of the world, therefore the world hateth you."[8]

---

[5] Hebrews 12:3.
[6] Ephesians 6:17.
[7] Ephesians 6:16.
[8] John 25:19.

Now I saw in my dream that before Pilgrim had been able to proceed half-way through the city, night overtook him. He began to despair of being able to reach the mansion where he had been directed to lodge, and which he had intended to make his resting-place for the night. Besides, the broad and open street which he had been pursuing, was now twisting and turning in crooked windings; and it frequently became so narrow as to create in his mind serious apprehensions that he must have lost his way. But when he ventured to make inquiry of the citizens and ask for their assistance in regaining it, he was treated with rudeness and incivility; for the Christian Graces and their residence were hated names among them, and their visitors were invariably treated with discourtesy.

Now I observed that the Lord Immanuel had appointed spiritual Watchmen — with the Lamp of Truth in their hands — to guide the feet of His people into the way of peace, and to direct erring travelers who had "gone out of the way."[9] But some of these Watchmen had been found to be unfaithful indeed. Many of them had no oil of grace in themselves; and consequently, their lamps burned with a feeble and sickly luster, and the trumpets which hung at their sides gave forth uncertain sounds. Some of the other Watchmen (during this time in which Pilgrim passed through the city) had covered their lanterns with so much painted glass and tinsel ornaments, as to greatly obscure the pure light of truth. But there were still some who were distinguished for their vigilant watchfulness; they were always faithful at their posts — "holding not their peace day nor night."[10] Since their lamps were liable to be dimmed by the smoke of the city, they constantly rubbed them with the Prayer-polish. And when any of the Zion-ward travelers — either through weariness, exhaustion, or sleep — fell down on the street, these faithful ambassadors of the Lord Immanuel were heard sounding their trumpets of alarm, and exclaiming, "It is high time to awake out of sleep, for

---

[9] Hebrews 5:2.
[10] Isaiah 60:6.

now is your salvation nearer than when you believed!"[1] As they met the Narrow-Way-men hurrying up the streets, sometimes they would accompany them for a little while, in order to whisper words of encouragement in their ears, if they saw that they were faint-hearted. At other times, these Watchmen allowed them to proceed, with the passing watchword: "ALL IS WELL!"

So I saw that Pilgrim observed an individual with a haggard look, running quickly up to one of these Watchmen; and he asked him, in great anxiety of mind, "Watchman! what of the night? Watchman! what of the night?"[2] The man's name was Anxious Inquirer; he had been awakened from a slumber of self-security, by the Trumpet of the Law — sounded by a Watchman whose name was Boanerges. From that moment, he had been hurrying from street to street, in a state of agitation; he had gone from Watchman to Watchman, with this question: "What shall I do to be saved?"[3]

"Have you found no one, poor man," inquired the individual whom he now so urgently addressed — "have you found no one to soothe your troubled heart, and to direct you to the Narrow Way that leads unto life?"

"None! None!" was the reply. "The unfaithful Watchmen that go about the city found me; they smote me, and they wounded me.[4] They tried to heal my hurt slightly, saying, 'Peace! Peace!' when there was no peace.[5] If you have any pity for a lost soul, please tell me what time of night it is; for I am beginning to fear that 'the night is too far spent!'[6] I thought, while I was hurrying along, that I heard the tolling of the midnight bell; and it seemed to say, as if with a living voice, 'Too late! Too late!' And the gloomy Watchmen who met me exchanged the same dismal watchword. Tell me — oh! Tell

---

[1] Romans 13:11.
[2] Isaiah 21:11.
[3] Acts 16:30.
[4] Song of Solomon 5:7.
[5] Jeremiah 8:11.
[6] Romans 13:12.

me: have I time yet to repent? 'Watchman! what of the night? Watchman! what of the night?'"[7]

"The morning cometh!" was the answer. "It is not yet come, but it cometh quickly. Although you are at the eleventh hour, yet do you see how the star of Hope still twinkles in the sky? But make haste, and follow me! Truly the night *is* far spent! Yonder bell will peal its last stroke before long – proclaiming that 'time shall be no longer,' and that the hour of repentance has fled!"

So I saw that Inquirer, under the guidance of this devoted ambassador, hurried through the crowd in the direction of the gate of the Narrow Way. The eye of Pilgrim followed them until they were out of sight. The promises on his shield reminded him of the glorious recompense awaiting such faithful watchmen as the one to whose guidance Inquirer had entrusted himself. "They that turn many unto righteousness shall shine as the stars in the firmament, for ever and ever."[8]

By this time, Pilgrim had arrived at the end of a narrow lane, which diverged into two different paths; and it became a matter of perplexity to know which one to select. As he stood there in indecision, he observed an individual coming up to him with a lamp at his side, similar to those that he had seen in the hands of the Watchmen. It emitted a feeble light; but it was sufficient, however, to show Pilgrim that the man was attired in armor, which appeared similar to his own. And the manner of his speech gave Pilgrim reason to suppose that he was once more to be cheered by the company of a Zion-ward traveler. But he was mistaken! This man had only a reputation of spiritual life, and nothing more.

His name was Professor; he had the Lamp of Profession in his hand, but he had no oil of grace to feed it; he had just enough light to distinguish him from his fellow-citizens, but not enough to let him see the way to the Celestial City. Although he had never entered through the Narrow-Way-Gate, he had contrived, at one time, to

---

[7] Isaiah 21:11.

[8] Daniel 12:3.

traverse (like many others) a considerable part of the way with his face Zion-wards. But he had never gotten farther than the town of Carnality, where he had taken up a permanent residence. Often he invited passing travelers to the Celestial City to visit him, and thus he had acquired a name for his hospitality. He was one of those with whom Pilgrim had already frequently met in his journey, and for whom he felt deep sympathy; because their pretended love for the Narrow-Way-men, and their alleged partiality for their King, made them hated by the Broad-Way-travelers. And all the while, they themselves had neither part nor lot with the subjects of Immanuel – either in their present privileges, or in their future glorious reward.

Pilgrim, after listening to Professor's conversation, availed himself of his offered invitation. And so, deferring his journey to the edge of the city until morning, he accompanied him to his residence to spend the night.

Upon arriving at the house of his new entertainer, Pilgrim found two guests already seated at his table – who, like himself, professed to be travelers to Immanuel's land. The name of the one was Antinomian, and the name of the other was Lukewarm. Antinomian did not have on so much as a shred of armor; in fact, he seemed to even glory in his state of imaginary freedom from the self-imposed burdens (as he called them) to which his fellow-travelers unnecessarily subjected themselves. Lukewarm was arrayed in something that resembled armor; but it hung so loosely upon him, and he talked so coldly of the Lord of the Way, and so slightingly of His blood-bought privileges – that it seemed to be a matter of indifference to him whether he entered the gates of the New Jerusalem or not.

Supper was concluded; and Pilgrim, being fatigued with the exertions of the day, retired to rest. He arose as soon as morning began to break; and although he was urged by Professor to prolong his stay, he dreaded to remain any longer in the company of those whose sentiments so little matched his own. He bid his entertainer farewell; and before they parted, he whispered in his ear some serious counsel about his imminent danger, and that of his guests. And then

Pilgrim hastened once more to run with patience the race that was set before him.

Now I saw that as he pursued the remainder of his journey through the city, he passed immediately under the walls of Free-thinker's palace – which he had observed in detail when he had entered the city. He hurried by as quickly as he could. Above the massive archway which formed the entrance, he saw these words emblazoned: "No soul! No judgment! No immortality! Death is an eternal sleep! Let us eat and drink, for tomorrow we die!" He shuddered as he heard the voices of the scoffers in the banqueting hall within the palace. They were blaspheming the name of the Lord of the Way, and saying, "Where is the promise of his coming? for since the fathers fell asleep, all things continue as they were from the beginning of the creation!"[9]

The doorkeeper of the palace, whose name was Ridicule, stood at the gate (as was his custom) in order to heap derisions upon all the travelers who passed by. He called after Pilgrim, and invited him to partake of Free-thinker's hospitality. He denounced all of the promises inscribed upon Pilgrim's shield as "cunningly devised fables"; and the Celestial City, with its alleged glories, as a dream. And he recommended that Pilgrim should return without delay, and resume his association with the Broad-Way-men. But Pilgrim only hastened his footsteps, and hurried more quickly past – replying thus to his words: "Truly, if I had been mindful of the country whence I came out, I might have had opportunity to have returned; but now I desire a better country, that is, an heavenly."[10]

Walking boldly onwards, Pilgrim at last reached the outer wall of the city; and with a joyful heart, he left its din and bustle behind him. Upon proceeding a little farther, he found himself standing in front of a gateway leading to an elevated mansion in the suburbs; and upon this gateway, he read this inscription:

---

[9] 2 Peter 3:4.
[10] Hebrews 11:15, 16.

"HERE ABIDETH THESE THREE: FAITH, HOPE, AND CHARITY."[11]

This was the place to which he had been directed by Piety and Devotion. It was the residence of the Christian Graces, who made it their delight to receive toil-worn travelers after their passage through the City of Carnality. They would wash their stripes, bind up their wounds, and supply them with necessary refreshments for completing their journey.

Sweet were the hours of conversation which Pilgrim enjoyed in this sacred resting-place! Sometimes their discourse focused upon the Lord of the Way Himself; sometimes upon the experience of travelers who had now entered into their rest; sometimes upon the glories of the Celestial City, whose shining gates – from the elevated situation which the mansion occupied – were in full view. On the top of the house was a balcony, where Pilgrim often resorted in company with Faith and Hope, who directed his eye through telescopes that were provided for the purpose of seeing the walls of the New Jerusalem.

Being replenished, after a temporary sojourn, with what was necessary for his journey; and having his shield and armor burnished anew with the Prayer-polish, which caused them to shine with dazzling brightness in the reflected beams from the Celestial Gate; Pilgrim once more found himself alone – a solitary traveler – hastening along the Narrow Way, with his back to the City of Carnality, and his face towards the City of Zion.

I saw that he continued to run, with eagerness and joy, the race which was still set before him – his path being like the "shining light, which shineth more and more unto the perfect day."[12] Indeed, the season of trials and changes was not yet over! Difficulties and temptations, and sorrows and discouragements were still there to remind him that the valley which he was in was – to the end – a Valley of Tears. But these only made Pilgrim long more ardently for the day

---

[11] 1 Corinthians 13:13.
[12] Proverbs 4:18.

when every tear would be wiped away; every pang forgotten; every sorrow ended; when the weapons of earthly warfare would be exchanged for robes of glory; and when faith would be swallowed up in sight, hope in fruition, and death itself in eternal victory!

Questions for Thought – Chapter Eleven

Why were the Pilgrims not allowed to pass by the palace of Mammon? What was the "costlier tribute" that had already been paid by the Lord Immanuel? See 1 Peter 1:18.

Piety and Devotion gave Pilgrim directions to go to the residence of the Christian Graces, on the other side of the city. But along the way, the citizens of Carnality became attracted to Pilgrim. What made him "stand out from the crowd"? In our Christian walk, do we tend to resemble the world; or do we "make a statement" that sets us apart — not only by the way we dress, but even in our daily lifestyles; such as what we say (or don't say) with our mouths, or what kind of activities we engage in during our spare time?

How do we distinguish between a true spiritual watchman and a false one? What was the difference between the lamps carried by each kind of watchman? If we understand their lamps to be the Word of God (Ps. 119:105), then what does this tell us about how spiritual watchmen or ministers ought to present the Scriptures to their audience? Should their lamps be tinted with worldly philosophy and man's opinions, or should the pure and simple Gospel light be allowed to shine in an unadulterated fashion?

Unfortunately, the Church is not immune from the ways of the carnal world subtly slipping in among her members. As we travel through life's pathway, we cannot completely avoid interacting with folks from the City of Carnality. But do we uphold our brothers and sisters by praying for them, so that they may not succumb to the world's enticements? Especially

John Ross MacDuff

in times when we may be physically separated from our true spiritual friends and companions, do we pray for the Holy Spirit to come alongside of them and strengthen and comfort them? And do you pray also for yourself, using the words of the Lord's Prayer: "Lead us not into temptation"?

Entrance into the Celestial City | 12

Now I saw in my dream that Pilgrim had approached near to the walls of the Celestial City; but there was still a dark valley intervening between them, which formed the only access to its gates. This valley was called the Valley of the Shadow of Death,[1] and it was similar in name and appearance to that which he had once traversed. And as he found himself about to enter it, he stood trembling with terror!

"Be thou faithful unto death," said a voice behind him; "and the Lord Immanuel will give thee the crown of life!"[2]

"Welcome! Welcome!" replied Pilgrim, beholding Faithful by his side – the Ambassador of the Lord Immanuel, who had so often appeared to him by the way. "Welcome, man of God! I greatly need your valuable counsel and companionship in such an awful hour."

"A Counsellor who is mightier than any earthly one is with you," was the reply. "Although He is unseen, the only Friend that can help you is already by your side. He Himself hath trodden this very valley before you; never yet has one of His travelers found Him to fail. A few brief moments more – and sorrow and sighing will flee forever, and you shall be in the presence of the Great King!"

"True! True!" agreed Pilgrim. "The brief sufferings of this present hour are not worthy to be compared with the glory that is about to be revealed.[3] One moment in yonder bright world will make me forget them all." And with this, he sung to himself one of the sweet strains which he had heard in the Palace of the Psalmist of Israel:

---

[1] Psalm 23:4.
[2] Revelation 2:10.
[3] Romans 8:18.

"Yea, though I walk through the Valley of the Shadow of Death, I will fear no evil: for thou art with me; thy rod and thy staff they comfort me."[4]

"Yes," said Faithful; "no tear needs to dim your eye. This hour which terminates your wanderings in a world of sorrow, is the commencement of a tearless immortality!"

"Amen! Even so!" exclaimed Pilgrim, as he seemed to be oppressed with the increasing gloom, and longing for the closing scene. "'Even so! Come, Lord Jesus!'[5] Come quickly! Lord Jesus, receive my spirit!"

Now I saw that they had arrived by the brink of a dark and swollen stream at the end of the Valley. A dense mist hovered all around, which temporarily obscured the glories of the Celestial City from their view.

"I feel a haze gathering around my eyes," said Pilgrim. "Tell me, can this be death?"

"Your warfare is now closing," said Faithful. "The gloom prevents you from seeing the portals of glory, although you are on their very threshold. The passage through this river will be over quickly! Before you plunge in, let your eye rest for the last time upon the shield of faith; and read there the promise of the Omnipotent One, Who will bear you through: 'When thou passest through the waters, I will be with you!'"[6]

"The darkness grows still deeper," said Pilgrim; "but although I cannot see, I think I feel the support of arms underneath me. Is it so?"

"These," said Faithful, "are the Everlasting Arms – with which the Lord Immanuel upholds His own covenant-people in their last struggle through the billows of death, so that it is impossible for them to sink."

---

[4] Psalm 23:4.
[5] Revelation 22:20.
[6] Isaiah 43:2.

"But hark!" said Pilgrim. "Although mine eyes are failing, and mine ears can do no more than catch up the sound of your voice; I think that I hear the notes of celestial singing close by me! The cadence of heavenly voices is falling upon my spirit!"

"It is the voices of the angels of God," replied Faithful, "who are waiting on the other side of the river to carry you into the presence of the Great King. It is the signal that the Lord Immanuel's last intercessory prayer on your behalf has ascended and been heard: 'Father, I will that they also whom thou hast given me be with me where I am, that they may behold my glory.'[7] And it is the token that your name is now registered among the citizens of Zion!"

"Farewell, then! Farewell!" cried Pilgrim – the last faltering words of earth escaping from his tongue, as he embraced in his arms the servant of his Lord. "Farewell! We shall meet in yonder bright world, where the Master Whom you serve will not allow you to lose your reward. Farewell, earth! Farewell, sin! Farewell, sorrow! Farewell, tears! Welcome, death! Welcome, Jesus! Welcome, heaven! Welcome, glory! Welcome, victory!" And with these words, Pilgrim plunged in; and the Ambassador of the Lord Immanuel saw his face in the Valley of Tears no more.

Now I saw that angels were waiting on the opposite side of the river, to conduct Pilgrim into the heavenly City. For a time, he was lost sight of in the deep waters. Billow after billow swept over his head. But at last, he was brought safely through; and thus he was welcomed by the angelic band: "Well done, good and faithful servant; enter thou into the joy of thy Lord!"[8]

Pilgrim found himself walking by the margin of a "river, clear as crystal, proceeding out of the throne of God and of the Lamb."[9] The golden palaces of Zion were reflected in its still waters; and trees – waving with eternal greenery, and distilling immortal fragrance – lined its banks. This river was called the River of the Water of Life.

---

[7] John 17:24.
[8] Matthew 25:21.
[9] Revelation 22:1.

Aged travelers and once toil-worn warriors reclined on its banks, and drank from its crystal streams. Many of these had been covered with dust, and others with blood; but in this peaceful river, every trace of pollution was purged away. And after washing their wounds and bathing their temples, they hastened to ascend the Hill of Zion. Death-divided relatives were seen crowding to meet them – wearing blood-bought crowns, and carrying harps of gold. Joyous indeed were the reunions!

Pilgrim had now arrived in front of the entrance to the City. The gate itself was of solid gold. The pillars which supported it were composed of jasper and onyx, and all manner of precious stones, which shone with a brightness that was dazzling to behold. Upon presenting the Charter sprinkled with the blood of Immanuel, which Pilgrim had received at the Narrow-Way-Gate; the angels opened to him the everlasting portals, exclaiming, "Thou shalt walk with the Lord Immanuel in white; for thou art worthy!"[10] And when he had been admitted, Pilgrim was overwhelmed by the blaze of glory which surrounded him! As he stood there – absorbed in his delighted

---

[10] Revelation 3:4.

amazement – another retinue of angels came rushing down from the throne. They were singing hallelujahs; and they had in their hands a crown of pure gold, which they placed upon Pilgrim's head, saying, "Thou art come unto Mount Zion, and unto the city of the living God; to the heavenly Jerusalem, and to an innumerable company of angels; to the general assembly and church of the firstborn, which are written in heaven; to God the Judge of all, and to the spirits of just men made perfect!"[11]

Now I saw that Pilgrim was carried away into the "third heaven," in company with these angels and saints, with shoutings and rejoicings. He passed along through worshipping ranks of angels and archangels, and cherubim and seraphim. As he got nearer and nearer to the eternal throne, their ascriptions of praise waxed louder and louder! When he had first entered the gates of glory, it seemed like "the sound of much people." As he ascended further, it became like "the voice of a great multitude." Higher still, it was like "the noise of many waters." And at last, as the glory brightened, it became like "the voice of mighty thunderings!" And so loud were the deepening anthem-peals, that it awoke me from my dream!

---

[11] Hebrews 12:22, 23.

Questions for Thought –
Chapter Twelve

What is represented by the dark valley that Pilgrim had yet to traverse before he could enter within the walls of the Celestial City? How could Pilgrim's frame of mind be described, as he was about to enter this valley? Would you say that you tend to think of the hour of death in the same way?

As Pilgrim was about to go into the valley, who appeared by his side? Faithful told him that there would be Someone Who would accompany him through this difficult time. Who was that Person? Jesus — the Author and Finisher of our faith (Heb. 12:1, 2) — has gone before us through the Valley of the Shadow of Death, and He came out victorious! Do you not believe that He will preserve each one of His children in safety, as they follow in His footsteps? What words of comfort may we read in the Shepherd's Psalm, which may be directly applied to our situation when we find ourselves passing through this valley? See Psalm 23:4.

To what did Faithful direct Pilgrim for comfort before he entered the dark river at the end of the valley? As Pilgrim passed through the dark river, why was it impossible for him to sink and perish? Do passages such as Deuteronomy 33:27 minister comfort to your soul, as you think about the hour in which you must pass through this same river?

What did Pilgrim have to hand in at the entrance to the City, before the angels opened up the gates for him? What was special about this Charter? Remember that since you have been washed and purified in the cleansing blood of the Lamb, heaven belongs to you! Admittance within its walls is a privilege that is guaranteed to each and all who have been redeemed by the

Savior's blood at the very entrance to the Narrow Way. O that every reader of this book may be washed clean from their sins and defilement, brought safely to their journey's end, and at last be ushered — as Pilgrim was — into the very throne-room of the One Who bought them with His own precious blood! May God grant that it may be so. Amen.

www.ingramcontent.com/pod-product-compliance
Lightning Source LLC
Chambersburg PA
CBHW062001040426
42447CB00010B/1855